101 Things For Kids To Do Screen-Free

DAWN ISAAC

PHOTOGRAPHY BY KATE WHITAKER

Kyle Books

An Hachette UK Company
www.hachette.co.uk

First published in Great Britain in 2020 by
Kyle Books, an imprint of Kyle Cathie Ltd
Carmelite House
50 Victoria Embankment
London EC4Y 0DZ
www.kylebooks.co.uk

ISBN: 9780857835291

Distributed in the US by Hachette Book Group, 1290 Avenue
of the Americas, 4th and 5th Floors, New York, NY 10104

Distributed in Canada by Canadian Manda Group, 664 Annette St.,
Toronto, Ontario, Canada M6S 2C8

Publisher: Joanna Copestick
Editorial Director: Judith Hannam
Editor: Tara O'Sullivan
Editorial Assistant: Sarah Kyle
Design: Louise Leffler
Photography: Kate Whitaker
Illustrations: Sarah Leuzzi
Production: Lisa Pinnell

A Cataloguing in Publication record for this title
is available from the British Library

Printed and bound in China

10 9 8 7 6 5 4 3 2 1

For Rosemary and Hilary – my wonderful support team. X

Try water gun painting

Plant a tyre garden

Create a space nebula

Compete in no-hands eating

Mix memory sand

Make a T-shirt bracelet

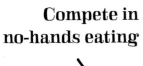

Draw outdoor chalk games

Make balloon creatures

Cook a mug cake

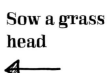

Sow a grass head

Contents

51. Make a washer pendant
52. Make balloon creatures
53. Create an autumn leaf picture frame
54. Freeze some hands
55. Launch a balloon rocket
56. Make a climbing mouse
57. Play consequences
58. Try cup weaving
59. Make a mini scarecrow
60. Try balloon printing
61. Compete in no-hands eating
62. Make a tape town
63. Dig a beach pool
64. Rustle up nachos
65. Hold wacky relay races
66. Mix memory sand
67. Make a mini lantern garland
68. Cut out paper snowflakes
69. Weave stick spider webs
70. Hold a thumb war
71. Create an outdoor race track
72. Fold a Chinese fan
73. Construct 3D stars
74. Make snack art
75. Play pebble games
76. Hang ice mobiles
77. Sow a grass head
78. Make savoury doughnuts
79. Play paper plate ring toss

80. Construct newspaper plant pots
81. Concoct potpourri
82. Make peppermint creams
83. Play halt
84. Thread snowflakes
85. Play beach mini golf
86. Make herbal bath bags
87. Try water gun painting
88. Create pebble pictures
89. Make a nature tic-tac-toe
90. Play Billy goat splash
91. Make a pomander
92. Mix carrot cake bites
93. Make pop-up cards
94. Play the table present game
95. Create garden art
96. Make a memo board
97. Plait wool dolls
98. Make drawer dividers
99. Build junk models
100. Fold a money shirt
101. Hold a night-time treasure hunt

About this book

Are you serious?

Will it hurt?

Is it even *possible*?

Yes, these are all reasonable things to ask when you see the words SCREEN-FREE.

And of course it must be painful and boring because your parents think it's a *Very Good Idea*. After all, they are always watching TV programmes about the dangers of screen time, or reading reports on their computers and phones about how children should spend less time... on computers and phones.

But it's okay. You can breathe. I have – for the sake of science – experimented with this terrifying "screen-free" concept myself. I have even forced children to undergo the same rigorous test conditions and I am happy to report that no serious long-term harm was noted.

Even more surprising – and you may want to sit down for this – they actually managed to enjoy themselves.

I know. This pretty much blows your current thinking out of the water, but it is true: screen-free time doesn't have to hurt. In fact, turn off your screens and you might find there are other things to do. Just off the top of my head I can think of 101 of them.

So how about experimenting yourself? Why not try walking on tin can stilts, making a magic wallet, cooking a mug cake, creating a mini-golf course or painting with water guns? You might even find you have fun at the same time.

Play down on one knee

YOU WILL NEED:
A TENNIS BALL (OR SIMILAR),
2 OR MORE PLAYERS

Don't worry, this is a game, not a suggestion. You don't need to spend the whole day shuffling along on one knee (unless you find that a particularly exciting idea – in which case I am going to have to question your sanity).

In fact this is a game to test your catching skills and requires nothing more than a ball (and two or more players).

Stand facing each other (or in a circle if there are three or more of you). Now you need to throw the ball to each other, but if there's a group of you this should be in no particular order – muddling it up keeps people on their toes.

If you fail to catch a ball that's thrown to you, it's time to go "down on one knee". Miss again and it's down on two knees, a third miss means one hand behind your back and after a fourth miss, you're out!

Luckily you have a chance to "earn back" your limbs and for each successful catch you can move back up – regaining an arm or leg, whichever you last lost.

Oh, and throws must be deemed "catchable" otherwise the thrower should have to try again or else "lose a limb" themselves – whichever rule you decide to play by.

The last one left in the game is the winner.

**Tip: You can add more levels to lengthen the game –
shutting one eye, or even having to catch lying down
makes an interesting challenge.**

Try sprouts

No, not like that. This is a game. Not a game where you throw Brussels sprouts and try to hit your brother's head (although, come to think of it, that does sound fun). Instead it's a simple but addictive game involving nothing more than pen and paper (oh, and a bit of mathematical strategy).

Begin by drawing two or more dots on a piece of paper. Now players take it in turn to draw a curve connecting two dots or drawing a loop and connecting a dot to it. Whichever is done, a new dot must be placed somewhere along this curve.

Each player takes it in turn to do the same following only these rules:

1. No line can cross another

2. No dot can have more than three lines going to it

The game continues until a player can't go – in which case the last player to add a line is declared the winner (and may now throw Brussels sprouts at the loser's head*).

*Okay, I'll admit it, I have completely made up this rule.

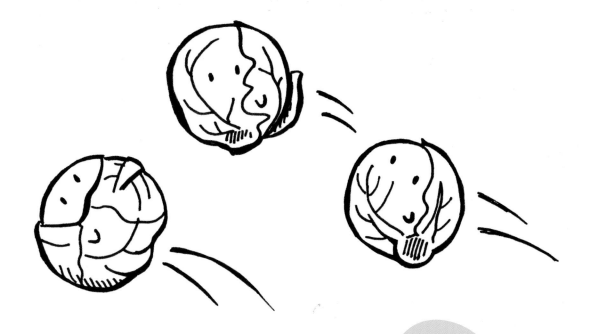

Tip: Adding more dots at the start makes the game longer and more complex.

A three-spot game of sprouts

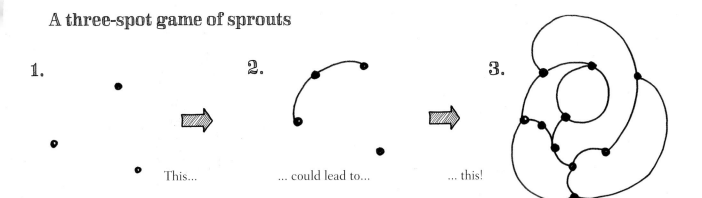

1.   ➡ 2.   This...   ... could lead to...   ➡ 3.   ... this!

Hold a toy swap

This is the perfect way to get hold of some new toys without having to wait for birthdays and Christmas, or doing anything as boring as actually saving your pocket money.

First, you're going to need to get your parents on board – but if they look dubious, throw in a few phrases like "responsible recycling" and "money-saving possibilities" and they'll soon toe the line.

Now you'll need to invite friends to your toy swap. Let them know the time and date of the swap and ask them each to bring about three to five toys they no longer want and would be prepared to trade. And while you're at it, you probably ought to write this down on an official invitation – let's face it, you kids aren't exactly known for your brilliant timekeeping or grasp of details.

When you all get together, take it in turns to hold up and "sell" your toy. I know you no longer want it, but you're going to need to remember why you once liked it or nobody's going to be interested.

When you've done your "pitch" and everyone's looked at the toy, people can start offering a swap. If you get several "offers" pick the best one, but remember, if nothing takes your fancy, you don't have to do the swap at all – and no-one needs to swap with you either.

Now the next person has a go – and you continue taking it in turns until all possible swaps are complete and you have a brand new set of toys to enjoy.

Oh, and as this could take a while, you may want to provide a few snacks (perhaps some savoury doughnuts, see page 164) – or smile sweetly at your parents and suggest they do this as you are "so busy hosting".

Tip: It is worth having an adult on hand just to make sure swaps are fair – and no-one trades their brand new, state of the art, super expensive game for something that came out of a cracker.

YOU WILL NEED:
OLD TOYS, INVITATIONS,
FRIENDS, PARENTS' PERMISSION

Play battleships

If you need a nice quiet game to play at the table that makes absolutely no mess, then try shooting torpedoes at battleships.

Hopefully you will have worked out that these aren't real torpedoes… or battleships. Instead you create your sea and set out your fleet on nothing more than a piece of paper.

Each player will need two grids, each 10 squares by 10 squares. You can draw these on a plain sheet of paper, although it's easier if you use squared or graph paper. Mark along the bottom with numbers (1–10) and up the side with letters (A–J) (see diagram).

Now place something between you and your opponent – a book propped upright or a cereal packet works well and old pizza boxes are ideal – so you can't see each other's plan.

You must now mark your battleships on one of your grids. These can run horizontally (side to side) or vertically (up and down) and you can add crosses or shading to show where they sit. The only rule is they can't be touching each other – even at a corner.

Each player should add one battleship (four squares long), two cruisers (three squares long), three destroyers (two squares long) and four submarines (one square each).

When your fleets are marked you take it in turns to launch a torpedo strike at your rival by shouting out a coordinate, for example "H5" (this is the square that lines up with 5 along the bottom and H along the side). If this lands in the sea it's a "miss" and your opponent gets a go, but if it lands on any of their ships they shout "hit" or, if it is the last or only square of a ship, "hit and sunk" – either way you get another go until you "miss".

The first one to sink all their opponent's ships is declared the winner.

Oh, and if firing on battleships sounds just a tad violent, please feel free to remodel this game in any way you see fit: "bomb the marshmallows", "hit the sausages" or "sink the pool noodles" would all work equally well.

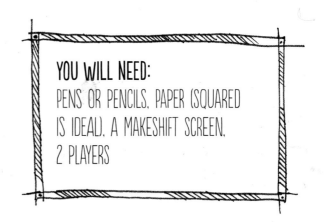

YOU WILL NEED:
PENS OR PENCILS, PAPER (SQUARED IS IDEAL), A MAKESHIFT SCREEN, 2 PLAYERS

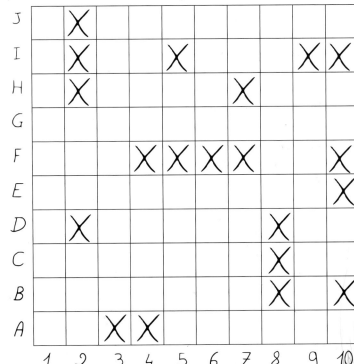

Tip: Keep track of your torpedo attempts and any ships you hit on the second grid so you don't repeat yourself and waste a shot.

Example grid

	1	2	3	4	5	6	7	8	9	10
J		X								
I		X			X				X	X
H		X					X			
G										
F					X	X	X	X		X
E										X
D		X						X		
C								X		
B								X		X
A			X	X						

Create chalk stencil art

These make incredibly impressive pictures, but here's the bit you want to keep quiet – they are *really* easy to make. Like I said though, keep that to yourself and just let people tell you what a brilliant artist you are.

First, decide what sort of picture you want to make. To create a Northern Lights masterpiece, all you need for a template is to tear along your paper or card to form hill shapes. Now lay this on a spare piece of paper and rub lots of chalk near to the edge. You can do this either all in the same colour or use different shades as you go. If you go over the edge it won't matter as your spare piece of paper is there to protect the table.

Now place your chalked-up stencil on your black paper and use your fingers to smudge the chalk upward in nice bold strokes. When you lift off your stencil at the end, you will see these look like magical lights in a night sky. If you reload your template with more chalk, you can add another range of hills to your artwork to make it even more exciting.

To make a cityscape, use exactly the same technique, but this time draw a city skyline on a piece of paper or card and cut this out. Again, you can use this more than once to create a busy city skyline. You can also add window details afterwards with white or yellow chalk.

And for a string of fairy lights, just make a light bulb template by folding over a piece of card, drawing half the light on one side and cutting it out to make a symmetrical shape. You can use a different chalk colour for each bulb and then add white chalk lines to string the lights together.

Tip: To stop your finished artwork smudging, you can coat it in hairspray.

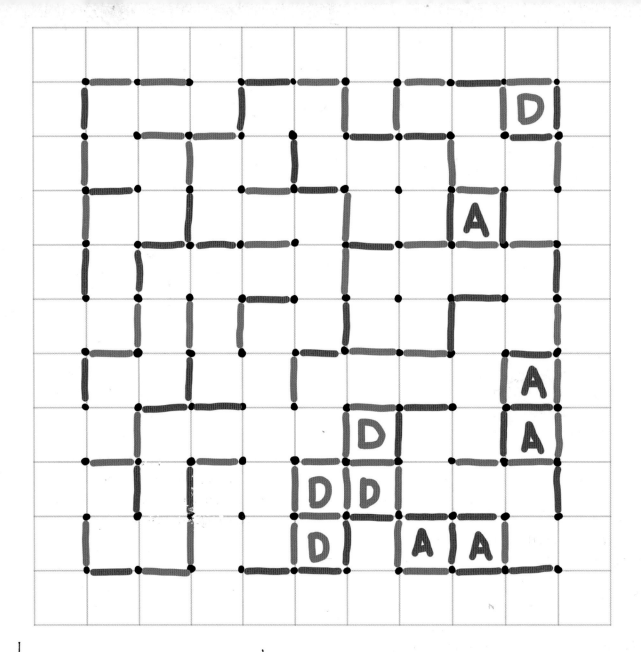

Tip: You can use symbols like a circle or a star instead of initials to claim your completed boxes.

Play dots and boxes

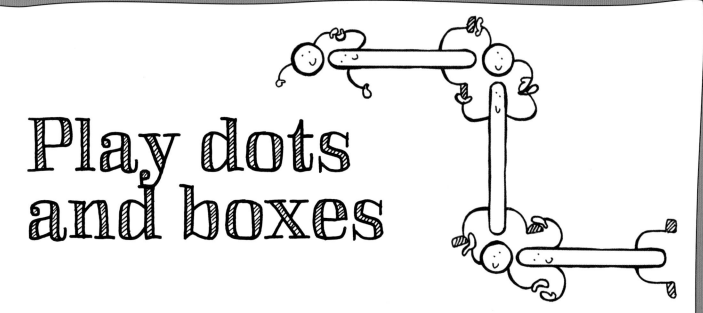

This is the perfect way to kill time when you're trapped somewhere very boring: waiting for a doctor's appointment, stuck in a traffic jam, listening to your sister's piano recital, looking at your homework – you get the picture.

You will, of course, need at least one other person to play with – preferably not someone driving a car at the time, about to launch into a rendition of "Für Elise" or supervising your homework. But apart from that, you're only going to need pencil and paper, which means this is a very easy game to create.

Begin by making a grid formed of dots – this is easiest to do on squared paper where you can place dots at each corner, but as long as the dots roughly line up, you can use any paper you like.

It should be at least 10 dots high and 10 dots wide, but you can make it any size (especially if this recital or traffic jam looks like it will last a while).

Now players take it in turn to add a line joining two dots. The aim is to try and "complete" boxes, which happens when all four sides are filled in, but not to allow your opponent to do the same.

If you do eventually spot a box with three lines completed, you can add the fourth. When you do this, make sure you write your initials into this box to claim it as yours. Oh, and each time you complete a box, you get to draw another line.

The game keeps going until all the lines are filled in – or the recital finishes – and then players count up how many "boxes" they each completed and the highest number wins.

Glue spider webs

Poor old glue, it only ever seems to get the supporting parts when it comes to crafting. It's always hidden behind card, or paper, or felt or pom-poms. Thankfully, we're about to give it a starring role.

First, find a thick piece of plastic film to glue onto. Recycling the clear plastic from packaging can work well for this.

You need a PVA glue bottle with a nice fine dispenser – school pack sizes are usually ideal. Now simply use your glue like a pen. By squeezing it gently, you can add a line – just make sure this doesn't have any gaps and stop squeezing just before you reach the end so you make a neat finish. Add another three lines – all crossing over at the centre to form a series of eight spokes for the base of your web.

Next, add curving lines between each of the spokes until you have reached the outer edge of the web.

If you want some added sparkle, shake on a little glitter – just as long as it doesn't hog all the limelight from the glue.

YOU WILL NEED:
SHEET OF THICK PLASTIC, PVA GLUE, GLITTER (OPTIONAL)

Now leave this for a few hours to dry and, when the glue has gone transparent, use your fingernails to carefully prise up the edge of the web before slowly peeling it off the plastic.

The web can be placed on windows or glossy painted surfaces where it will stick all by itself, awaiting its craft Oscar award and preparing an emotional acceptance speech.

Plant a tyre garden

Ever wanted to create new worlds in your own back garden?

What do you mean "That sounds like hard work"?

How about if I said it'll only take you an afternoon or two?

Yep. I thought that might do it…

First, you're going to need an old tyre. And yes, I know that doesn't sound too promising, but stick with me, okay?

Give the tyre a wash with some warm, soapy water (outside is best as grown-ups tend to frown when you take old car parts into the bath with you) and then you can decorate. Make sure you lay down an old cloth or cardboard for protection and wear old clothes. You can then use a paint roller or brush to apply some acrylic paint to the tyre. It's best to apply lots of thin coats and let them dry in between.

To add a base, take an old potting compost bag, cut along the sides to open it up, place it on soft ground like a lawn and then use a gardening fork to make holes in it. Now move the tyre to where you want your world to be and place the old compost bag at its base so it covers the bottom and up the sides before trimming it to size.

You now need to fill your tyre with potting compost, firming it down as you go, before deciding what sort of world you want to create.

If your tyre is in a mostly shady area, you can plant one or two small ferns (check they won't grow too large). These not only have lovely leaves, but they're also older than almost any other plants so are perfect for a prehistoric world. Just add some large boulders, a moss-covered floor and a few toy dinosaurs.

In a sunny spot, try planting some succulent plants such as sempervivums and sedums. If you add a little bit of geotextile fabric, cutting holes for the plants, you can add a layer of sand on top and create your own desert world, perhaps with a few sidewinder snakes. You could add gravel and rocks to create dried-up riverbeds.

You could even sow grass seeds – or see if a grown-up will let you use a piece of turf – which you could trim low to create a savannah. If you sink a small bowl you can even use this to create a watering hole for toy elephants, tigers and hippos.

YOU WILL NEED:
OLD TYRE, OLD CLOTH OR
CARDBOARD, PAINT ROLLER
OR BRUSH, ACRYLIC PAINT,
OLD POTTING COMPOST BAG,
SCISSORS, GARDEN FORK,
POTTING COMPOST, SMALL
PLANTS, GEOTEXTILE FABRIC
(OPTIONAL), PROPS AND TOYS

Tip: Ask at garages and car repair shops for old tyres you can use.

Make chalk paint

Sometimes things are so small they're of no use at all.

Stop looking at your little brother like that – I was talking about chalks!

Yes, when you've used them so often they're just a little stub, it can be tempting to throw them away, but don't! Because old ends of coloured chalks are perfect for recycling as chalk paint.

Begin by sorting your old chalks into colours. Now put all of one colour into the plastic bag, and place it inside an old towel. Take it outside and then take your hammer or mallet (which is when your parents start looking super nervous) and bash the towel. Unfold it every now and then to check on the chalk and keep going until it has been turned into dust. Now you can place it in an old container – an old muffin tin is perfect – and move onto the next colour.

When you've made your dust, hand the hammer or mallet back to your parents so they can stop panicking. Now dribble a little water into each dust-filled compartment of the muffin tin, or your containers, and mix it carefully with a teaspoon until nice and smooth and not too thin – in fact it should look and feel very much like paint.

Now you're ready to start chalk painting outside, ideally on a nice clear and smooth surface like a path or driveway. If you want to stop the colours mixing, it's best to use a different paintbrush for each one. And it's a good idea to keep a small jug of water close to hand as the chalk paint can dry out quite quickly – especially in hot, sunny weather. And maybe keep a nice long, cool drink of lemonade close to hand as well – just so you don't dry out either.

Tip: If you don't have chalks, you can mix a cup and a half of cornflour with a cup of water, divide it into a muffin tin and add food colouring to each. This is particularly good for splatter painting.

Fold and sail a boat

YOU WILL NEED:
PAPER, STICKY TAPE
(OPTIONAL)

These boats are great to sail in a bath, but even more fun down a stream. If you want to do this just remember you need to take a well-behaved grown-up with you – you know, the ones who are seen but never heard – to make sure you stay safe.

There are two versions – one faster and easier, and one that is slightly trickier, but which makes a better boat. The choice is yours (but yes, I will judge you if you don't even attempt the trickier one).

Simple paper boat

Fold your paper in half from top to bottom. Now fold it from side to side and then unfold it so you can see the crease.

Fold down the top corners to meet the centre crease. Next fold up the strip at the bottom before turning over and doing the same on the other side. Congratulations – you've made a paper hat! But we're not done, so you can stop patting yourself on the back now.

Open the hat up and then flatten it down in the other direction to form a diamond shape, slipping the end flaps under each other to tidy them away.

Now fold the bottom of the diamond upward, turn it over and do the same on the other side, giving you a triangular shape.

Next open this up, like you did for the hat shape, and again flatten it down in the other direction to form another diamond.

Finally, take hold of the points at the top of the diamond and pull them sideways to form a boat. Ta da!

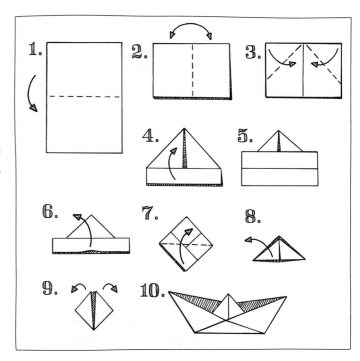

Sampan boat

Lay your paper out so the longest side is at the top and bottom. Now fold it in half lengthways by lifting the bottom edge to meet the top edge to form a long rectangle. Now take the top layer and fold it down to the bottom, turn it over and do the same on the other side so you are left with an even thinner rectangle.

With the double folds at the top, bend down the top right corner to meet the bottom edge, making a right-angled triangle. Now fold the top right corner down again to meet the bottom edge. Repeat these two folds on the left-hand corner. Fold down the top edge. Turn over and repeat this for the other side.

Now stand it up to form a boat-like shape, flatten down the middle fold and then hold the edges and very carefully turn these inside out. And ta da – your boat is done!

Tip: Add sticky tape to the base of your boats to make them waterproof.

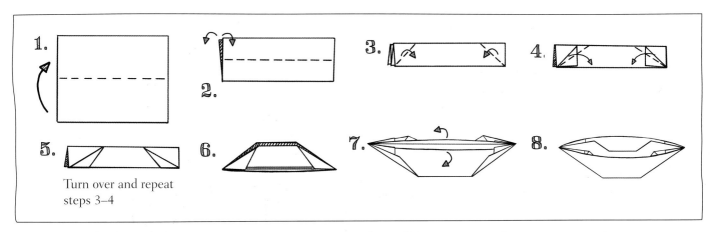

1.

2.

3.

4.

5.

Turn over and repeat steps 3–4

6.

7.

8.

Tip: Use newspaper sheets to make a bigger version or try using other material such as foil or greaseproof paper.

Create cardboard costumes

Poor cardboard: it has so much potential and yet, what do people keep turning it into? Boxes. That's what. Well, it's time to right this wrong and set cardboard free, because the truth is, cardboard is the perfect material to make almost anything – including amazing costumes.

You can decide the costume you want to create in advance, maybe even making some sketches, or else you can simply get going and see what happens.

Whichever method you choose, begin by opening out your box, but be careful if it is attached with staples as these can be quite sharp.

Next cut some construction strips from your cardboard, which should be the width of a ruler. These are then used to form the basis of any costume. For example, a strip around the head with two more strips attached front-to-back and side-to-side makes the perfect foundation for any headpiece from a helmet to a top hat. Two strips made into loops and attached to a straight cardboard section as wide as your back gives you armholes so you can put on a back-mounted costume, whether that's fairy wings, a dinosaur's spines or anything your imagination desires.

And a strip across your chest and one across your back with two side strips attached makes a base for a costume that covers both your front and back like a body of armour or a robot's torso.

When you are attaching strips, or anything else, you need to use a thin layer of PVA glue. You have to give this a few minutes to work so it's easiest to hold the cardboard together with clothes pegs or under some books, until it's well stuck.

The thinner your cardboard, the easier it is to cut, but it can also lack strength. If this is a problem, cut out your shape, then draw around it two or three times more on the cardboard and then cut these out and stick all the layers together. This also works well with accessories such as swords and shields or wands and axes.

YOU WILL NEED:
CARDBOARD OR CARDBOARD BOX, SCISSORS, RULER, PENCIL, PVA GLUE, CLOTHES PEGS, PAINTS (OPTIONAL), YOUR IMAGINATION

Tip: For added colour, you can paint your cardboard costume when it's finished.

Make a friction rocket

We may be crafting a friction rocket here, but there is no need to limit yourself to this model. You can create anything you would like to see climb great heights from card: a spider, a superhero, your granny (seriously, never underestimate the ability of grandparents to scale the sides of buildings – they just don't tend to do it when you're watching).

To begin, cut out the shape of your rocket. It is helpful to design it on paper first, folding the sheet in half and drawing one side along the folded edge. This means that when you cut it out it and open it up, you will have a perfect symmetrical template to use. Then simply draw around this carefully onto a piece of card and cut it out.

Add decoration cut from different coloured paper or use pens to add the details. When you're happy with the rocket, turn it over and use sticky tape to attach two equal lengths of straws – approximately 4cm (1½in) long – to the back. Make sure they both point inwards a little toward the top of your rocket (see photo).

Now you need to thread a piece of string or wool in a loop – up one piece of straw and then down the other piece of straw. If you have a large needle you can thread it through using this. Alternatively, you can put a very small piece of sticky tack on the end of the wool so it's not much wider than the wool or string itself. This adds more weight so it will help pull the length through as you drop it into the straw.

The length of string or wool needs to be just over twice as long as the highest point you want to have your rocket reach. You can then tie a large bead to the ends of the string or wool, or simply fold a piece of sticky tape over each one, just to stop the rocket from sliding off.

To work your rocket, hook the middle of the string over something like a coat hook or door handle. If it's too high for you to reach, ask a passing, long-limbed grown-up to help. Now, start pulling the string, one side at a time and watch your rocket (or spider, or superhero… or granny) rise!

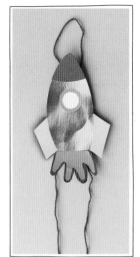
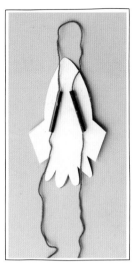

Front   Back

Tip: Using wider straws will
make it easier to thread
through the wool or string.

Try shadow drawing

YOU WILL NEED:
A SUNNY DAY, CHALK,
A MODEL

"Put your hand higher. No, I meant lower. Now touch your nose. Oh, and balance on one leg."

Yes, the best thing about doing shadow drawings is getting people to do ridiculous things in the name of art. But it's also a remarkably easy way to make some great pictures.

First you'll need a sunny day – shadows are fussy like that – and a nice open space no-one will mind you drawing on – driveways or playgrounds are always good.

Now get a friend, or someone you can boss about in the family, to create interesting shadow shapes – maybe an action shot, a classic "teapot" pose, or a wave. Or how about bringing in some props? When you're happy with the look, it's time to get your chalk and draw around the shadow edge. Just be careful to do this without blocking out the sun or you'll lose the line you're tracing.

Oh, and make sure you try this at different times of day so you can experiment with different shadow shapes as the sun moves across the sky.

When you're done, you can add more details, colour it in with more chalks or chalk paint (see page 26) or simply make your sister's nose look twice as big just to annoy her.

Tip: If you have no willing volunteers, you can always get a piece of paper and a pencil to trace the shadows of your favourite toys instead.

Make your own face paints

You're gorgeous. I know. But if you ever get bored with staring at your beautiful reflection, how about going for a bit of a change? May I recommend trying to look like a clown, or a cat, or a ladybird, or a rainbow or… well pretty much anything really. Because that's the fun of face paints.

But if you don't have a set to hand, there's no need to panic (or return to staring at yourself in the mirror). Instead you can create your very own.

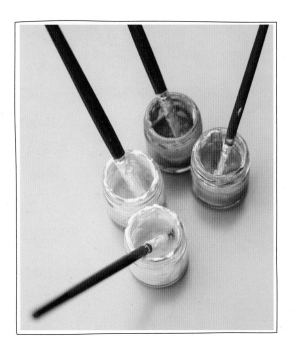

Begin by adding to a bowl:

4 teaspoons cornflour
4 teaspoons lotion
2 teaspoons flour
2 teaspoons water
2 teaspoons oil

Mix them together until you have a smooth paste. Now divide this between several small pots – ones with lids are good if you want to store them for a day or two in the fridge. Finally, add a few drops of different food colouring to each until you have the range of paints you need.

Now you can start on your creation. It takes about half an hour to dry so try not to smudge it while you wait. Also, be careful not to get it on your clothes as the food colouring can stain and grown-ups tend to get a bit annoyed about that sort of thing.

If you are doing this with a friend you can paint each other's faces or else you can use that other good friend to help – your mirror.

YOU WILL NEED:
BOWL, TEASPOON, CORNFLOUR, FACE OR BODY LOTION, PLAIN FLOUR, WATER, VEGETABLE OIL, SMALL POTS (PREFERABLY WITH LIDS), FOOD COLOURING, BRUSHES, MIRROR

Tip: You can wash off the paints with soap and water when you are done.

Tip: Use different sized squares and different coloured paper to make a variety of flowers for a bouquet.

Folding a petal

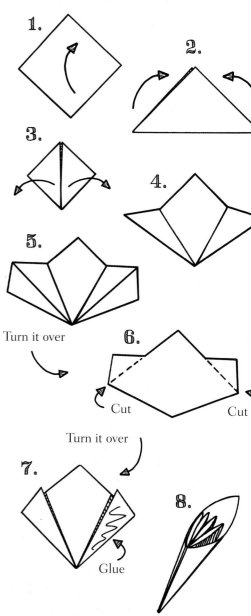

1.

2.

3.

4.

5.

Turn it over

6.

Cut   Cut

Turn it over

7.

Glue

8.

Tip: If you have a sequin or plastic jewel, this makes a perfect decoration for the centre of the flower.

Fold paper flowers

YOU WILL NEED:
PAPER, SCISSORS, GLUE, CLOTHES PEGS, KEBAB SKEWERS

Flowers make a wonderful "I'm-sorry-I-made-a-mess" present, "I'm-trying-to-get-back-in-your-good-books" present or, I guess, even just a present-present (but let's face it, the first two are probably the ones you need most often).

So, why not make a few everlasting paper flowers to have on hand? You know… just in case.

For each flower, you'll need to have five squares of the same size. If you take a sheet of paper and fold one corner over so the edges line up, press the crease in firmly and then trim off the excess at the bottom, you will have one very large square. You can then fold this top to bottom and side to side and cut out the four squares that this makes. Do this as many times as you need.

For each petal, fold your square opposite corner to opposite corner to make a triangle (diagrams 1–2). Now bring each outside point of the triangle to meet the point at the top (diagrams 2–3). Fold back from the middle point, press the crease (diagrams 3–4) and then lift up the flap, open it out and bend it back flat to form a kite shape (diagrams 4–5).

Do the same on the other side, then turn over your shape and cut off the small triangles that poke over the top (diagram 6).

Turn back over, then fold over the sides so they line up (diagram 7) and then place a little glue on one section and attach it to the other so it forms a rolled petal shape (diagram 8). It needs to stay like this until the glue dries. You could force your little brother or sister to hold it, but it is easier, (and causes fewer complaints) if you just use a clothes peg instead.

When you have made five petals, join a group of two and a group of three together by adding a little glue along the edges and holding them with clothes pegs. When they are dry, use a little more glue and clothes pegs to glue the two sections into a full flower shape.

You can slide a kebab skewer into the base at the centre to form a stem and, if you want to add some leaves, fold some more paper, draw on a half leaf shape and cut it out.

Try book folding

Now let's get something straight: the very best thing you can do with books is read them. Lots. But if… and only if… you have read a book so many times that it's starting to fall apart, then this is definitely the second best thing you can do with it.

Fold a hedgehog

Yes I know, "folding a hedgehog" sounds painful for both you and the hedgehog, but thankfully no animals will be harmed in the making of this creature.

For your hedgehog you need about 180 pages, so you can use a short book or separate this number from a longer book. Fold the first page in half lengthways, then turn down the top corner so it meets the centre of the book and turn up the bottom corner about a third as much (see diagram).

Repeat for each page. You can check you have the bottom fold lined up by folding it over the page you have already done to ensure it's the same size.

To finish the transformation, cut out two front paws and a nose from black card and stick them on using PVA glue. You can then use white card with black circles drawn to stick on as eyes.

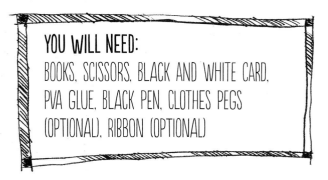

YOU WILL NEED:
BOOKS, SCISSORS, BLACK AND WHITE CARD, PVA GLUE, BLACK PEN, CLOTHES PEGS (OPTIONAL), RIBBON (OPTIONAL)

Fold a vase

For this you will need most of a book (about 300 pages or more). On the first page fold the bottom right corner up to meet the centre of the book and create a triangle shape. Now take the edge of this triangle shape and again fold it into the centre and crease. Finally, fold over the overlapping triangle at the top so it doesn't stick out (see diagram).

On the next page fold down the top right corner to the middle of the book to form a triangle. Now fold up the bottom right-hand corner to meet the bottom of the first triangle. Finally, fold in the outside point this has created until it meets the intersection of the two triangles (see diagram).

Now just alternate these two folds for the rest of the book.

When you're done, remove the outside covers and stand up your vase. You can tie a ribbon around the top to help keep the shape together as well as for decoration. And why not try inserting paper flowers (see page 39) into the middle of the vase?

Folding a hedgehog

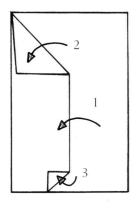

Folding a vase

Page 1

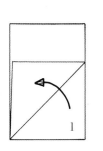
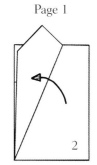
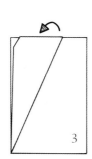

Page 2

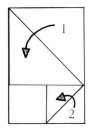
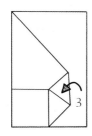

Tip: Use clothes pegs to hold groups of folded pages together to stop them getting in your way as you fold more.

Learn some riddles

Riddles are great at stretching your mind, making you think in different ways, displaying the cleverness of language. But let's be honest, the best bit about riddles is when you know the answer and get to be really, really smug about it.

So now we've got that straight, why don't you learn a few corkers that you can torture your friends with?

Q: The more you take, the more you leave behind. What am I?
A: Footsteps

Q: I'm light as a feather, yet the strongest man can't hold me for more than five minutes. What am I?
A: Breath

Q: What runs, but never walks, often murmurs, but never talks, has a bed but never sleeps, has a mouth but never eats?
A: A river

Q: If you are running in a race and you pass the person in second place, what place are you in?
A: Second place

Q: If I have it, I don't share it. If I share it, I don't have it. What is it?
A: A secret

Q: How many months have 28 days?
A: All 12

Q: What belongs to you, but is used more by others?
A: Your name

Q: What goes up and never comes down?
A: Your age

Q: How can a man go eight days without sleep?
A: He only sleeps at night

Q: What gets wetter the more it dries?
A: A towel

Q: The more there is of me the less you see. What am I?
A: Darkness

Q: What goes up the hill and down the hill, but despite it all, just stands still?
A: A road

Q: What grows when it eats, but dies when it drinks?
A: Fire

Q: Which is heavier, a kilo of bricks or a kilo of feathers?
A: They weigh the same – a kilo is a kilo

Build an insect hotel

The good thing about insects is they're not that fussy. Forget room service, heated towel rails and reception desks, these critters just want a place to lay their heads (or tails… or wings… or exoskeletons).

Still, they are a bit particular about wanting peace and quiet so the first thing you need to do is locate a spot in the garden that's sheltered and away from busy paths. Now put down four bricks – two in each line – the same width as your lengths of wood. Place your wood across the top and hey presto, the first floor is completed. Keep doing this, adding bricks one or two layers high and then wood to bridge the two.

When you've constructed the final floor, add an extra piece of wood to the back section and then place on roof tiles. The angle will help the water to run off.

Now it's time to create some rooms, or habitats, that visitors might appreciate. You could put a curved roof tile in the basement – perfect for frogs or toads to hide under, or get old cardboard tubes and fill them with hollow plant stems or rolled-up corrugated card so small insects can shelter in the gaps. You could ask a grown-up to drill holes in logs – great for solitary bees – or simply add some old leaves, pieces of bark and pine cones for bugs to make use of.

Finally, make sure you visit regularly to check if anyone's moved in – but just be sure you're quiet and don't move things around. You may not be able to see them, but there are tiny "Do Not Disturb" signs hanging everywhere!

Create a space nebula

Creating space in your bedroom – that's tricky. I mean it probably involves tidying for starters. Recreating *part of* space in your bedroom – that's a lot easier.

In particular we are going to create a nebula, otherwise known as a giant interstellar cloud of dust and gases where stars are born or die. Like I said, it's a lot easier than tidying up.

Begin by adding some water to your jar – to about a quarter or even a third of the way up. You can then add some tempura paint or food colouring to this and mix it with a long-handled spoon or a skewer before pushing in some cotton wool. If the cotton wool is in balls, just push a few down until they reach the top of the water, or if it's from a large roll, pull off smaller sections and use them in the same way. Once you're happy with this, you can sprinkle some glitter on top, and use your spoon or skewer to make sure this also moves down the side of the jar.

Add further layers in different colours by mixing similar amounts of water and food colouring or paint in a second jar or mug, soaking this up with more cotton wool, and then spooning it into the jar. Again, add glitter to these layers as you go.

Once you have reached the top of the main jar and you're happy with the look, put the lid on your jar and place it somewhere it can be admired. Or else just pop it alongside all the other junk in your bedroom.

Tip: You can use acrylic paint to decorate the jam jar lid so it also looks suitably "intergalactic"... and less like it once contained mayonnaise or chocolate spread.

Build fairy houses

YOU WILL NEED:
THE OUTDOORS, NATURAL MATERIALS

Don't ask me why fairies can't build their own houses. They're probably too busy granting wishes or partying with the pixies and sprites. But whatever the reason, I'm sure they'll be very grateful for your architectural skills!

The rules – if indeed "making fairy houses" needs rules – are that all elements should be natural. And, of course, it needs constructing outside as that is where fairies feel most at home.

You can gather materials from the garden or out on a walk – hedgerows and parks are basically interior design shops in fairyland. Moss can become a carpet, an upturned shell is a perfect washbasin and leaves make wonderful blinds and curtains. But why stop there? You could add some sand by a puddle and you have a private beach, get creative with twigs and make an outdoor gym or how about a helicopter pad (you know, for when their wings need a rest)?

And while you're at it, you could build a few fairy shops, a fairy hotel or maybe even a fairy school. After all, if *you're* forced to go, I don't see why fairies should get off so lightly.

Tip: Fairies get easily bored, so do feel free to remodel their homes on a regular basis.

Tip: You can swap the vanilla essence for a teaspoon of lemon juice and lemon zest for a tangy alternative.

Make a mini cheesecake

So this is not a cake *and* it's not really made of cheese. Confused? Don't worry. All you do need to know is it's delicious, and it's ALL yours.

Yes, that's the joy of creating mini puddings like these – you are perfectly entitled not to share them with anyone.

Begin by putting your digestive biscuits in a freezer bag and then use the rolling pin to squish them backward and forward until they are broken into crumbs.

Place your butter in a plastic bowl and put it in the microwave for 10 seconds at a time until it has melted. Now add the soft brown sugar and the crushed biscuits and mix them all together thoroughly. Spoon this mixture into the bottom of the glass, pressing it down to form a layer and then place it in the fridge to chill.

Whisk the whipping cream in a bowl until it is thick enough to stand up in soft peaks. In another bowl mix the cream cheese (yes, I know this is cheese, but it's not "cheesy cheese" so my first point still stands, okay?) with the caster sugar and vanilla essence before adding the whipped cream and gently mixing them together. You can now add this on top of the biscuit base, smoothing it gently with the back of a teaspoon. Finally, decorate your

cheesecake with fresh berries or sprinkles – or maybe both. It's your pudding, after all.

Now the hardest part: put the glass back in the fridge and let it chill for at least half an hour. And if you need to distract yourself while you wait, well… you can always make another cheesecake, can't you?

Perhaps this one could even be for someone else?

Don't worry – it's okay. I'm joking!

YOU WILL NEED:
2 DIGESTIVE BISCUITS, FREEZER BAG, ROLLING PIN, 15G (½OZ) BUTTER, 3 PLASTIC MIXING BOWLS, 20G (¾OZ) SOFT BROWN SUGAR, WOODEN SPOON, A SHORT GLASS, MICROWAVE, WHISK, 30ML (1FL OZ) WHIPPING CREAM, 50G (2OZ) CREAM CHEESE, 10G (⅓OZ) CASTER SUGAR, A FEW DROPS OF VANILLA ESSENCE, BERRIES OR SPRINKLES (OPTIONAL)

Play kick the can

This is a game mash up: it's a little bit of Hide-and-Seek, with some added Capture the Flag and a dollop of Tag on the side. Oh, and of course, you also get to kick a can. What's not to love?

To play the game you ideally need a fair bit of space and in the middle of this you put an empty can (because full ones can hurt your toes and ones half-filled with baked beans get a bit messy). Now the person who is "it" counts to an agreed number while everyone else runs off to hide.

"It" then has the job of hunting down players and, if they are tagged, these unfortunate souls are thrown into "jail" which needs to be in plain sight of the can.

Other players try to kick the can before they can be tagged. If they manage this, all the jailed players can immediately run free.

"It" wins if they can get everyone in jail. However, if there are lots of people playing it can be a bit much for a single person so you can have two or more people playing the part of "it".

Tip: If you don't have a can you could use a plastic bottle part-filled with water so it doesn't blow away.

52

Make a magic wallet

Making this wallet will almost certainly encourage grown-ups to hand you large amounts of money. And if that isn't magical, I'm not sure what is.

To pull off this amazing feat you first need to construct your wallet. Begin by measuring and cutting two rectangles from your piece of card, both 15cm × 9cm (6in × 3½in), and then four strips from your paper, each 15cm × 1.5cm (6in × ⅔in).

Now lay two of your strips as shown in diagram 1, running behind one rectangle and overlapping onto the other. Use sticky tape to attach the overlapped pieces to the left-hand rectangle, then bend over the other ends and tape them to the right-hand rectangle.

Take the other two paper strips, cross them over each other and use glue or tape to secure them in the middle. Slip this cross under the left-hand rectangle as shown in diagram 2 and secure two of the overlapping ends to the right-hand rectangle before bending over the other ends and taping them to the left hand-rectangle. Now fold the wallet shut.

To neaten up the wallet, cut a final two rectangles – also 15cm × 9cm (6in × 3½in) – and stick these to the outside so you can't see your taped ends.

Now for the magic: ask a grown-up if you can borrow a bank note to put in your wallet. Explain that it's a wallet with special powers and then slip the note under the cross-shaped strips in the wallet. Carefully close the wallet, incant some magical lines, wave your hands in a mystical fashion and then open it, *but from the other side*. Amazingly, the note will have jumped from one side of the wallet to the other!

As an added trick you can suggest going out to celebrate with some milkshakes or perhaps a trip to the sweet shop, where, for your next trick, you can see your parents' money completely disappear!

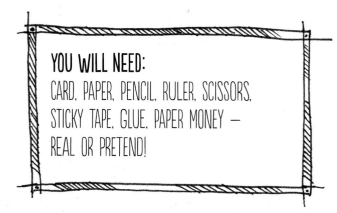

YOU WILL NEED:
CARD, PAPER, PENCIL, RULER, SCISSORS, STICKY TAPE, GLUE, PAPER MONEY — REAL OR PRETEND!

Tip: You can make a tougher version of this wallet by using cardboard wrapped in duct tape for the main body of the wallet and adding ribbons instead of paper strips.

Making the magic wallet

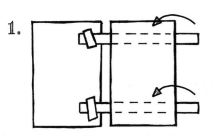 1. → 2. 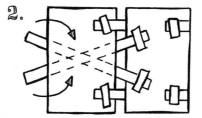 → 3.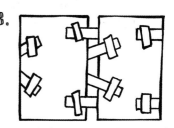

Learn a card trick

The second thing on that "You will need" list is the hardest. Magicians are many things: show offs, posers, fans of cloaks and top hats, and keepers of bunny rabbits, but they are not, I repeat not, blurters. That's because the moment a magician tells everyone exactly how they did a trick, it stops looking like magic. So keep quiet, okay?

That's better.

Now let me tell you exactly how to do this trick.

Me? A blurter? I don't know what you're talking about!

First, you need to shuffle your pack of cards. You can do this as long and elaborately as you like. Maybe even get your bunny rabbit to help. But the important thing is to make sure you catch sight of the card on the bottom of the pack and remember it.

Now fan them out, face down, toward your adoring fans, and ask someone to pick a card without letting you see it, then tell them to memorize it before putting it on the bottom of the pack.

You can now cut the pack – or get an audience member to do this – by lifting off the top half and then putting the bottom half back on top of it. This means the chosen card is now hidden somewhere in the middle of the pack.

Except… it's not hidden from you. This is because when you go through the pack pretending to somehow read your audience member's mind, their chosen card will be on top of your memorized card from the bottom of the pack. Not that you'll tell them that of course. Because you're not a blurter.

YOU WILL NEED:
A PACK OF CARDS,
NOT TO BLURT

Tip: If you are careful and can remember roughly where the cards are, you can cut the pack more than once to add to the "wow" of the trick.

Coil magazine bowls

A word of warning: if you use an old magazine for this craft you will be considered a creative and resourceful child who knows the value of recycling. However, if you use the magazine a grown-up has just purchased from the shop, you will not. And in fact you may need to run and hide. Fast.

So now you've triple checked no-one wants the magazine any more, you can start to pull out the pages. You need only half a page at a time so take a few sheets and line them up. Next, gently bend them over twice so you have a manageable size and then use scissors to first take off any rough torn edges, and then cut all the pieces in half (see diagram).

Now take each half sheet and use either a thick kebab skewer or a rounded pencil and start to roll from the bottom corner upward at an angle. Try to keep the roll relatively tight and then secure the final end with a small piece of sticky tape. You can then pull your pencil or kebab skewer out and flatten your straw-like paper.

When you have made plenty of these strips you can start constructing your bowl. Begin by coiling the first strip as tightly as possible and then, when you're nearly done, slot the next strip inside the end, secure with tape, and carry on coiling. If you need to take a break or make new strips, just secure the end with a piece of tape stuck on lightly.

When your coil is as large as you wish your bowl to be, stick on the last strip tightly. Now make sure you keep the centre of your swirl flat to form the base of your bowl and then begin to slowly pull up the outer coils to form the sides. Do this very gently and slowly to make sure you don't accidentally unravel your coil.

Finally, place the bowl on an oil cloth or greaseproof paper and paint it inside and out with PVA glue. This will help the coil keep its shape and add a protective gloss to the outside.

YOU WILL NEED:
AN OLD MAGAZINE, SCISSORS, THICK KEBAB SKEWER OR ROUNDED PENCIL, STICKY TAPE, OIL CLOTH OR GREASEPROOF PAPER, PVA GLUE, PAINTBRUSH

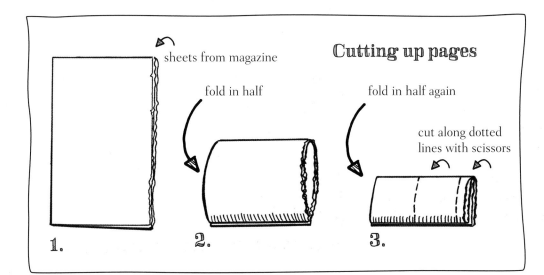

sheets from magazine

Cutting up pages

fold in half

fold in half again

cut along dotted lines with scissors

1.

2.

3.

Tip: To make sure the rim of your bowl is nice and level, you can turn it over and gently push on the edges until they look balanced.

Become a knot-tying master

These are all incredibly useful knots for surviving in the wild. If you have no plans to trek in the wilderness they can still be useful for joining things together, tying things up… or making jewellery. Admittedly that's less "life and death" dramatic, but as I say, still useful.

Square knot ⬇

Right over left then left over right.

Mostly useful because it's easy to remember, but also to tie bundles of things together like firewood… or lengths of knot-practising rope.

1. Cross the two ends of the ropes

2. Pass the end of one rope through the loop of the other

3. Pull the ends to tighten

4. Knot is complete

Sheet bend ⬇

This is better than the square knot at tying two ropes together, especially if you have different thicknesses of rope.

These instructions might make it simpler:

Make a loop in one end. The rabbit goes out of the hole, around the tree and then back under its path.

What do you mean "where's the rabbit?" The rope is the rabbit. No, there isn't really a tree. The other piece of rope is the tree. And, yes, the first rope is also the path. Complicated? I don't know what you're talking about!

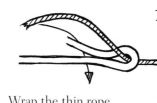

1. Pass the thin rope through the bend you have made in the thick rope

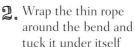

2. Wrap the thin rope around the bend and tuck it under itself

3. Hold the end of the thick rope and pull the thin rope to tighten the knot

Bowline

This makes a non-slip loop at the end of your rope. This can be useful for rescuing people who have fallen down a deep hole or just suspending your bag of snacks up a tree so your little brother can't nick them. You know, all of life's important skills.

Just remember:
"Loop the rope to make a hole
Then go through its back and around the pole
Over the top and through the eye
Pull it tight and let it lie."

Yeah, I know there's no need to "let it lie", but it rhymes so let's just leave it there, okay?

Make the loose end nice and long in case it slips.

1. Make a loop in your rope and then pass the end of the rope through this

2. Now pass the end behind the top of the rope and through the loop again

3. Hold the loop and the end of the rope and pull to tighten

4. The knot is made

Lark's head or cow hitch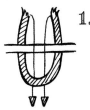

This should not be used to tie anything to a lark's head, or a cow, but it is very useful if you want to attach something to a loop, like a pendant to a necklace (see page 110).

1. Make a bend in the rope and place it behind your support

2. Thread the ends of your rope over the top of your support and then through the loop

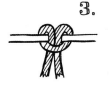

3. Pull to tighten

Clove hitch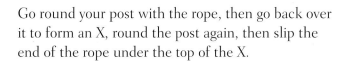

This is very useful to tie things to round posts or to start lashing two posts together (which is invaluable in that essential art of constructing mini scarecrows – see page 126)

Go round your post with the rope, then go back over it to form an X, round the post again, then slip the end of the rope under the top of the X.

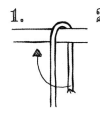

1. Hang rope from the support

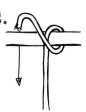

2. Loop around the support with the end

3. Thread the end of the rope back under the X shape it just formed

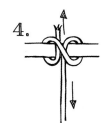

4. Pull to tighten

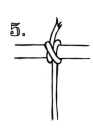

5. The knot is complete

YOU WILL NEED: ROPE OR STRING

Craft T-shirt bracelets

T-shirts don't always have a long life – you grow out of them, stain them, rip them or simply refuse to wear the one that has "Mummy's Little Cutie Pie" emblazoned across the front. Thankfully, they are the perfect candidates to be upcycled as these brilliant T-shirt bracelets.

First, you need to use your scissors to remove the hem at the bottom, and then cut strips about 2cm (¾in) wide. If you then pull these, they will curl in at the sides.

For a simple plaited bracelet, hold three of these strips together in a clip and then bring the strip on the right into the middle, then the strip on the left into the middle. Keep repeating this pattern until you have a plait long enough to go around your wrist. Unclip it, tie the two ends together tightly and cut off any excess. If you are an expert at plaits you can also try other versions such as the four-strand plait or fishtail.

Alternatively, you can join several strips together. Do this by bending over the ends of two strips and snipping a slit in both with your scissors. Now pass the end of the top strip through the two holes from the bottom and pull it tight. You can keep adding more and more strips like this until you have a length about 1.5m (1¾yds) long.

Now, holding the end of the strip with your thumb pass the thread behind your index finger and in front of your middle finger, then around behind your middle finger and in front of your index finger. Finally, wrap a loop of the strip around both fingers at once. Now lift up the loop at the base of your index finger, pass it over the second looped layer and off the top of the finger. Do the same on the middle finger. Now pass another loop of fabric around both fingers and again lift the lower loop over it on first your index finger and then your middle fingers.

Slowly you should start to see a woven strand appearing between your fingers. When this is long enough to go around your wrist, lift the last two loops off your fingers and carefully thread the material strip through both and tighten. You can now tie this in a bow with the other end of the bracelet.

Tip: If you want to hide any messy plaited ends, you can cut a rectangular strip of fabric and wrap this around the join, sticking it in place with PVA glue (hold this firm until it has stuck).

Fold tissue paper pom-poms

To make these it's best to use decorative tissue paper rather than the sort you blow your nose on. Especially not *after* you've blown your nose on it. Unless, of course, you want pom-poms with an added green motif… and germs.

First you can prepare your wire. Cut a section about 15cm (6in) long, bend it in half and then twist just below the bend so you create a small loop at the top with two long "legs" below. Now place this on one side.

Lay down your full-size sheet of tissue paper and fold it in half, then open it up and cut along the line. Put the two sheets on top of each other, carefully lining them up, and this time fold both over, unfold, and then cut along the line. Do this step one more time so you are left with eight sheets of a similar size. Alternatively, if you want to make a bigger pom-pom, use two full-size sheets to start with and just fold and cut twice to get your eight sheets.

Carefully pile your eight sheets together so they are lined up and begin to concertina fold from one of the shorter sides to the other. You should aim to make around 8–10 folds in the sheets so you are left with a long, thin, rectangular shape.

Bend your shape in half to find the middle, then take your wire and place the "legs" either side and twist the ends to hold it tight before bending over the twisted ends so they lie flat.

Finally, to add more texture to the edge of your pom-pom, use scissors to cut the ends of your rectangle – either rounding them or adding a point (which is slightly easier to cut).

Now for the magic. Open up the tissue paper on either side of your wire to reveal a fan-like shape and begin to separate a sheet of paper at a time. Be very careful as you do this because the tissue paper can easily rip.

When one side is completed, work on the other. It can take a bit of practice and tweaking to get the pom-poms to look well rounded, but when you are happy with them, you can thread a ribbon or some thread through the wire loop and hang these beautiful decorations wherever you wish (although ideally not near someone with a very bad cold and a tendency to sneeze).

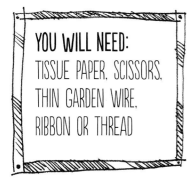

Tip: If you don't have decorative tissue paper you can actually use normal tissues. Just make a pile of 5–6 and follow the instructions opposite. Be extra careful in separating the layers as they are even more delicate.

65

Make and break codes

What's the best thing about writing in code? Driving grown-ups crazy of course. They will inevitably think these detailed secret messages are a plot to overthrow the adult world, when really, you've just written "Your feet stink".

Pigpen cipher

This is a very old code – yes even older than your parents – but unlike them, it's still remarkably useful.

All you need for this is the Pigpen Key (see below) and then you simply replace each letter with the corresponding shape of the key – so NOSY PARENTS would be translated like this:

Cipher wheel

This is a great way to make a complex code, as long as you and your friend have identical wheels.

To make your wheel, cut the central circle from one paper plate and then bend it in half in both directions to find the centre, which you can mark with a pencil. Now line it up on top of the second plate, put an eraser or lump of sticky tack under the centre and push a sharp pencil through the middle of both to make a hole.

Using a protractor, take the middle circle and mark every 10 degrees along the edge before using a pencil and ruler to mark these lines from the centre to the outside.

Place the circle back on the plate and use a split pin through the middle to attach the two. Now on the middle circle write all the letters of the alphabet and in the spare spaces write the numbers 1–9 and a question mark. Holding the central circle still, draw the lines out further onto the bottom paper plate so you have 36 segments here too. Now write the letters and numbers again but this time thoroughly muddled up. Just make sure you copy them down in the exact same order when you make your friend's wheel.

Now all you have to do is decide on the "key letter". This might be the first or last letter on your message. So if this is a T, you need to line up T on the outer circle with A on your inner circle. When this is done, you can match the encoded letters on the outside to the correct letters from the inside wheel to crack the code.

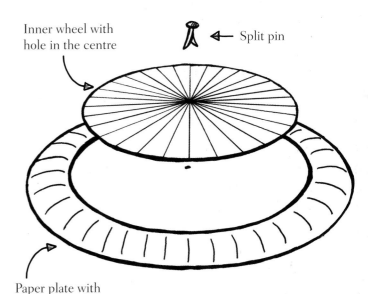

Inner wheel with hole in the centre

Split pin

Paper plate with hole at centre

Tip: Try to make up your own code using rules that only you and your fellow code breaker know.

Tip: If you want a "glitzier" feather, you can also use PVA glue to add sequins, stars or other decorations.

YOU WILL NEED:
BIRDS' FEATHERS, SCISSORS, INK, ACRYLIC PAINT AND FINE PAINTBRUSH OR ACRYLIC PAINT PENS

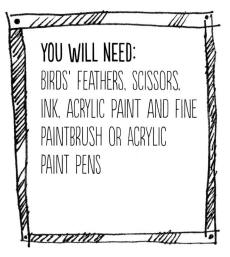

Making the quill

Cut 1

Cut 2

Craft a quill

This is the perfect craft if you want to pretend you are living "in the olden days". It's also a lot less painful than recreating the bad teeth, daily hardships and early deaths. Yes, it wasn't all "fun times" in centuries past, but at least the writing tools were cool.

To make your authentic quill, you first need to find a good-sized bird's feather, or preferably a few. Parks and hedgerows are a useful place to look, but thankfully birds exist pretty much everywhere so just keep your eyes peeled (not literally – that's getting a bit medieval again).

When you get your feathers home, give them a gentle wash in warm soapy water. When they are dry, you need to take your scissors and make a diagonal cut at the end (see diagram) and then a second cut up the centre of the longest side (this is where the ink flows down). This can be tricky, which is why it helps to have more than one feather to experiment on.

Dip your quill into the ink and test out how well it writes on a piece of paper, and if it passes this quality control check you can get decorating. Use acrylic paint pens or acrylic paint and a fine brush to add some colour to your feather. Have fun trying out different patterns and techniques, although you may find it easiest to paint or colour using the natural lines of the feather as a guide.

Make sock creatures

The most brilliant minds have been able to solve many mysteries of the world and even space, but still, there is always one question which eludes them: where do all those socks go? And perhaps we'll never know the answer…

Still, while there appears to be an endless supply of odd socks, you might as well do something with them. And what better than creating octopuses and snowmen!

Socktapus

Roll up your sheet of paper or card to form a funnel at the top of your sock and then pour in the rice to fill up the "head". Use an elastic band to hold the base of the head and then tie it tightly with a piece of string, wool or thread before removing the band.

Now cut up from the opening to just below the "head", spread it flat and then cut again to form two legs. Cut along both of these to form four legs, and finally cut along these four to form eight equal legs. If you then pull each one they will curl around the edges making them more like tentacles.

Finally, use PVA glue to stick on a pair of googly eyes or simply draw some on with a permanent marker.

Tip: For longer lasting decorations you can use thread to sew on buttons and ask a grown-up to hot glue the eyes.

Snowman

Cut the foot off a long white sock so you are left with a tube. Use an elastic band to close off one end and then turn the tube inside out so the band is hidden.

Add rice (as with the socktapus) until you are happy with the size of your snowman's body, and secure the end with an elastic band. Now pinch out a section of the sock on either side of the body and twist an elastic band onto each one to form arms. You can then tie these with wool or thread and remove the band.

Add more rice in the end to form the head and then use an elastic band to secure the top of the tube. Cut half the foot end off another sock and roll up the bottom edge to create a hat and place this on the snowman. Now cut a long section from the rest of the sock to make the scarf. Finally, use PVA glue to attach eyes and buttons to the snowman or simply draw these on with a marker.

YOU WILL NEED:
PAPER OR CARD, OLD SOCKS, RICE, ELASTIC BANDS, WOOL, STRING OR THREAD, SCISSORS, PVA GLUE, GOOGLY EYES, PERMANENT MARKER, BUTTONS

Fold an origami frog

If you've always wanted a pet frog, this is the one for you. After all, real frogs are tricky – what with them being wild creatures and avoiding human beings wherever possible. This one though is happy to be tamed, has slime-free skin, needs no slug-heavy diet and best of all, will turn somersaults whenever you want.

If you're using special origami paper, start by folding it in half. If you're using ordinary paper you just need to measure and cut a rectangle twice as long as it is wide, such as 20cm × 10cm (8in × 4in).

Now follow the folding steps opposite.

When your frog is completed you simply place it on a surface, push down on its back legs and release. The frog should leap into the air and, if you're lucky, do an entire somersault before landing back on its feet. If not, it might simply need bribing with a few slugs.

Folding – step by step

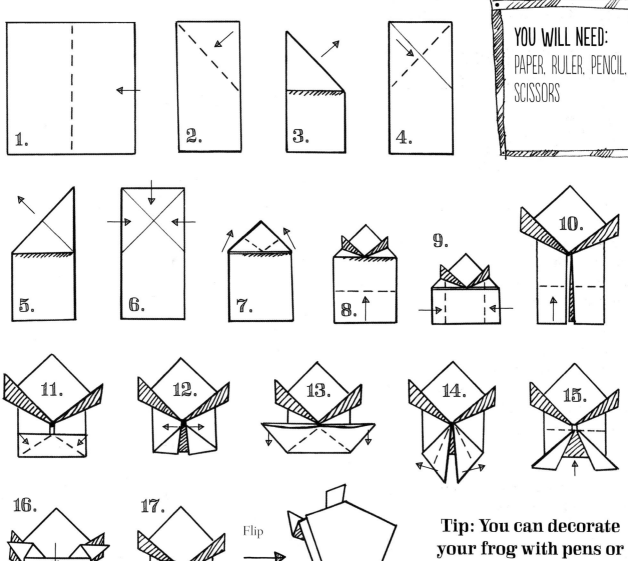

YOU WILL NEED:
PAPER, RULER, PENCIL, SCISSORS

1.

2.

3.

4.

5.

6.

7.

8.

9.

10.

11.

12.

13.

14.

15.

16.

17.

Flip

DONE!

Tip: You can decorate your frog with pens or add some googly eyes. You can also make them in any colour you wish. Yet another benefit over the real thing.

Tip: If you plan to make lots of frogs, make a rectangular template of card so you can draw around this onto paper again and again.

73

Cook a mug cake

Those grown-ups who use mugs to sip dull tea or coffee are missing a trick. Because the best thing to do with a mug is bake a cake in it. Obviously.

Start by getting a good-sized mug (350ml/12fl oz) – if it's smaller than this you might want to cut your ingredients back a little. Oh, and make sure there's no metal on it – even as a pattern. Microwaves get quite cross about metal.

Now measure out your butter into the mug and put this in the microwave. Heat it 10 seconds at a time until the butter is melted, then crack the egg into it and add the milk before whisking it all together with a fork until it's thoroughly mixed.

Next add the sugar and flour along with the vanilla essence, mix again with the fork until it's relatively smooth and then put the mug on a plate (to collect any spills) and put it in the microwave to cook for 2 minutes at 800 watts or 1 minute 45 seconds at 1000 watts… (I know, just ask the grown-ups about this bit – that's what they're good at, understanding microwave settings – oh, and sipping coffee.)

If the cake sinks a lot as soon as you open the door, then it's not quite cooked, so pop it back in and cook for bursts of 15 seconds until it no longer sinks much. Then, as soon as it's cool enough, tuck in.

Or, and here's the best bit, just use this as a starting point. The joy of mug cakes is it's easy to experiment and create all sorts of recipes. Instead of using four tablespoons of flour, use three and add an extra tablespoon of something else – how about some berries? Or mashed banana? Or grated carrot? Or ground almonds? Or glacé cherries? Or cocoa powder? Or sultanas? Or a mix of these?

You could swap the caster sugar for brown sugar or demerara. Or replace the butter with vegetable oil.

You could add a small pinch of ground cinnamon, or ginger or nutmeg.

And, of course, you could throw in some mini marshmallows and chocolate chips. I mean seriously – is there any recipe not improved with those? Exactly.

YOU WILL NEED:

2 TABLESPOONS BUTTER, MUG, MICROWAVE, 1 EGG, 1½ TABLESPOONS MILK, FORK, 2 TABLESPOONS CASTER SUGAR, 4 TABLESPOONS SELF-RAISING FLOUR, 1 TEASPOON VANILLA ESSENCE, PLATE, ALL SORTS OF OTHER INGREDIENTS (OPTIONAL BUT FUN)

Play spoof

Don't panic. I know I said you'll need "maths" but really all you need to know is your three times table. What's more, there could be sweets in it for you. See. I knew that would do the trick.

Begin by giving all players three coins, or three small objects or – and here's the best plan of all – sweets! Now everyone puts their hands behind their backs and without anyone seeing, transfers some, all or none of their three things into their right-hand fist and then puts this into the centre.

The youngest player goes first. They have to guess how many items are held altogether in everyone's fists. So if four of you are playing that could be any number from 0 (known as "spoof") to 12 (which is three times four. See – it was easy really). When they have guessed, the person on their left goes next. And then the person on their left, until all have guessed. The only rule is you can't repeat a number someone has already selected.

When everyone has guessed, you all open your fists and the number is counted. If anyone guessed correctly, they can drop out and then play resumes with the next person on the left going

first. And, of course, as there are only three of you, the guess will be anywhere between 0 and… come on, three times three… yes, 9.

It gets quite strategic, especially when there are only two of you left in and you're trying to bluff your opponent. And if you fail, and find yourself the last one standing, it can be fun to have a bunch of forfeits already written up so you can pull one out of the jar. Sorry, let me rephrase that. If you win, and one of your friends is the last one standing, it can be really fun to make them do a forfeit. Yep. That's what I meant.

Tip: If you play with sweets, you can let the first player out eat one of them, or, if it's you, maybe all three of them.

Set up an outdoor lounge pit

Getting out the paddling pool sounds like such fun, doesn't it? Well, until you realize it takes ages to fill, and then the sun's gone in, and that the water's a bit chilly, and finally that, horror of horrors, someone might ask you to help empty it at the end of the day. I know, it's an outrageous suggestion!

But how about using it without actually adding water? Because the thing is, paddling pools are capable of leading a double life – as inflatable lounges.

Simply blow up the pool – using an electric pump, or a helpful grown-up, makes this job a lot easier. Now place it wherever you fancy – sun or shade – but preferably not on or near anything sharp.

Then all you need to do is fill up the pool with lots of comfy blankets on the bottom as well as pillows and cushions around the side for you to lean against.

If you've got friends over this makes a great outdoor lounge pit to sit in and just chat, or you can make it your own little cosy spot, maybe taking some of your favourite books and snacks with you to keep you going. And if you do this, take a tray out too as it makes a great ground-level coffee table.

If you place your lounge pit on a lawn, it's really easy to pull it to a different spot if you decide you want a change of location. And at the end of the day, just wrap all your cushions in a blanket to carry them inside, and turn over your pool to keep it dry. After all, you might have another busy day lounging around tomorrow.

Tip: If the inside looks a little dirty, just wipe it out with some damp cloths before putting in blankets and pillows.

Make stress balls

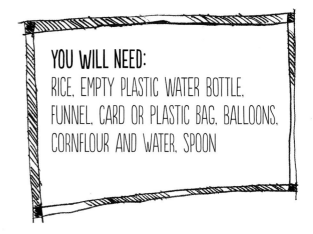

YOU WILL NEED:
RICE, EMPTY PLASTIC WATER BOTTLE, FUNNEL, CARD OR PLASTIC BAG, BALLOONS, CORNFLOUR AND WATER, SPOON

These balloon creations are perfect for juggling but thankfully they also make great stress balls. And, believe me, after failing to learn juggling, and knocking over that priceless vase in your attempts, you will definitely be feeling stressed.

First, measure out your chosen filling. Rice is particularly good for juggling balls. Measure 80g (3oz) and then add this to an empty plastic water bottle either by a wide funnel or folding a piece of card and using it as a chute. You could also try putting it in a plastic bag, twisting the bag loosely shut, and pushing this through the mouth of the water bottle before shaking out the contents.

Now stretch your balloon over the neck of the bottle, turn the bottle upside down and squeeze. You will need to keep pulling gently on the balloon and using your fingers to encourage the rice down the neck to get it into the main body of the balloon. When you have, tie a knot in the neck and cut off any excess.

Now take another balloon, cut off the neck and then put the first balloon into this, tied-end first so no messy ends are showing. You can repeat this again to add further strength to your juggling ball.

For the perfect stress ball recipe measure out 60g (2½oz) of cornflour and then pour on 45ml (1¾fl oz) of water. Mix this slowly with a spoon, folding the mixture over from the bottom to the top. When it's as smooth as you can make it, pour it slowly via a funnel into the squeezable bottle and fill the balloon in the same way as you did for the rice. Again tie the end when you're done, cut off any excess and then add another balloon section or two on top for added strength.

And finally, when your parents walk in and see the mess you have left behind, just hand them one of the balls and instruct them to start squeezing.

Tip: You can add a different colour balloon section as a top layer to make a two-tone ball.

Tip: As a shortcut you could add your rice to a small plastic bag, twist it shut, cut off any excess, then stretch a bottom balloon section over it. You can then add more balloon sections over the top as before.

Construct a tinfoil river

There are probably very important lessons to be learned with this project – you know, about gravity, soil erosion and water transport. But I'm guessing it will really just be about you getting soaking wet while trying to find the weirdest thing you can think of to float down your river. Yep. Thought so.

If you have a natural slope to your garden or drive, that makes a great start as the water will automatically flow in that direction. If it's all a bit flat, then you can add in some height of your own – maybe starting your river on a slide, or mounding up some soil in the garden and beginning it there.

To make the river itself put two long lengths of tinfoil on top of each other. Using a double layer means you have more protection from punctures and rips. Now shape this tinfoil so you have sides to your river. You can also mould it so it winds around the garden a little. Just try to make sure the end of the river runs into a part of the garden with plants that will appreciate the water coming their way.

Now place your garden hose at the start of the river and turn on the tap, but not too much. You should see the water flowing along the length of your river. If there are any bits that are leaking, add another section of tinfoil underneath, and if there are points where it overflows, adjust the path of your river until it works.

Now you can have fun sailing all sorts of things down your river, including homemade boats (see page 28), but really anything that floats – sticks, corks, balls, plastic ducks, it's up to you.

YOU WILL NEED:
ROLL OF TINFOIL, HOSEPIPE, OBJECTS TO FLOAT OR SAIL, STONES

Tip: If you want to use less water, you can shape your tinfoil into a circle and just fill it up once.

Tip: You can add stones along the river to change its flow and make obstacles to sail around.

Tip: Recycled mini jam pots make great little pots for lip balms.

Mix your own lip balms

These are perfect for keeping your lips protected in cold and windy weather. Also, they work well if you want to pretend you have just eaten a slice of cake or an enormous chocolate bar every time you lick your chops. Which is, of course, equally important.

First, take a teaspoon or two of petroleum jelly (or however much you need to fill your mini pot) and place it in the bowl. Now you can add your flavouring. Food flavourings – everything from vanilla and orange to pistachio and peppermint – are ideal as anything food safe is going to be fine on your lips. Just add two or three drops to your mixture. If you don't have any to hand, you could use a little cocoa powder (for a chocolate flavour) or honey (for surprise, surprise, a honey flavour).

To make it look a little more exciting, use food colouring. Again, just a drop or two is fine – you don't want to be walking around with bright blue lips. This is also an ideal way to recycle old lipsticks. Just cut off a tiny bit and mix it in to give yourself a tinted lip balm.

Tip: You can use coconut oil as a base instead of petroleum jelly if you prefer.

When you have thoroughly worked in your flavours and colours, spoon the mixture carefully into your presentation pot and smooth it down with the back of the spoon. Finally, put on the lid, wipe down the pot and add a sticky label to the top to let people know what to expect – "Chocolate chops lip balm" or "Strawberry and vanilla smackeroos" or "Pistachio pout". You get the idea.

YOU WILL NEED:
SMALL BOWL, TEASPOON, PETROLEUM JELLY, FOOD FLAVOURINGS, FOOD COLOURINGS OR OLD LIPSTICK, SMALL CONTAINERS OR POTS WITH LIDS, STICKY LABELS AND PENS

Make tin can stilts

First things first: you had better check your tin cans are the same height, otherwise you're about to make some very wonky stilts and that's not a good look. Also, remember the taller the cans, the taller the stilts. Coffee canisters or even paint tins can be used to make bigger and stronger versions.

Next, take your tin cans outside and ask a grown-up to help you use your hammer and nail to make two holes in the bottom of each one, near the edge of the side and opposite each other. This will leave some sharp edges on the inside of the can, so to smooth these out a little, take one or two large pebbles or stones, pop them in the can, cover the top with your hand and shake it hard up and down. As they knock against the edges of the holes the stones should smooth out the worst parts, but it is a good idea to ask a grown-up to double check there are no sharp bits left.

Next, cut two equal lengths of string or twine – each twice as long as one of your legs.

Thread one end of the string down each hole in a can. Pull them through far enough so you can make a square knot or sheet bend (see page 60) to tie the ends together and then pull the top of the loop until it tightens inside the can.

When you've done both you are ready to test out your stilts. Balance a foot on each, holding the loop of string, pulled tightly, in each hand. Now you need to lift the string and your foot one at a time, until you have mastered the art of… walking. Well yes, I know you had mastered this, but walking 20cm (8in) higher up in the air is trickier than you think, so less chatter, more practice, okay?

Tip: You can decorate your cans by priming and painting them, or sticking on card, coloured tape or stickers.

Craft a no-sew pouch

These are the perfect place to keep all sorts of little things stored away safely: little figurines, small building blocks, doll's accessories, dice and tokens…you know, pretty much everything that's usually just strewn across your floor.

Begin by laying a dinner plate on your old T-shirt and drawing around it carefully with a pencil before cutting it out.

Now lay a smaller plate on top of the T-shirt circle, and use this to help guide you to make pairs of marks 2cm–3cm (¾in–1¼in) in from the edge at the top and bottom and both sides. Now make two lots of similar marks between each of these, as though you were marking the numbers on a clock (see diagram).

Take off the plate and use the scissors to snip a hole at each mark (easiest done by folding over the fabric at this point) about 0.5cm (¼in) long.

Next, wrap a short piece of sticky tape around one end of your string or twine – this will stop it fraying and make it easier to thread. Pass the string in and out of each pair of "snips" until you have threaded the entire circle.

Take a mug or cup – something that will give you a smaller circle, and draw around it once on your card and twice on your paper before cutting these out. You can now stick the decorative paper to either side of your card before slipping it inside your pouch as a hard base.

Finish by threading each end of your string through either hole in a large button or by threading beads onto each end. Whichever method you choose, add a knot to the end of your strings so the beads or button can't fall off.

And now you have a useful pouch… so you had better start picking things off your floor to fill it.

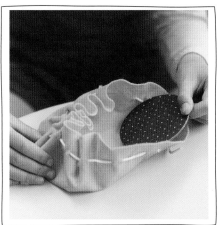
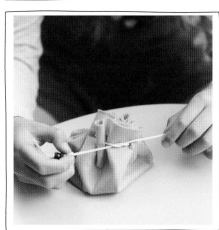

Tip: You can also use felt or fleece to make these pouches (as they won't fray) and if you have cord this works well to thread the tops.

Make a no-sew pouch

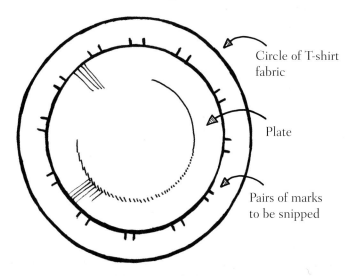

Circle of T-shirt fabric

Plate

Pairs of marks to be snipped

Play stop the bus

As you only need pencil and paper to play – and the ability to shout "Stop the bus!" – this is a great game to keep you entertained when you're out and about. Except perhaps if you're actually on a bus. That could be a bit confusing for everyone. Especially the driver.

You begin by each player drawing six columns on a piece of paper and then adding six rows beneath it. On the top row, from right to left, add five different categories – these could be anything you want from "girls' names" to "fruits" or "things made of metal" or "things Dad has broken this week" – it's really up to you. To make sure it's fair, players could take it in turns to volunteer ideas or draw them from a hat.

Now on the far left-hand column on the second row, you need to write a letter from the alphabet. You could simply start at A, or you can have a player run through the alphabet silently in their

head until someone says "Stop" – with whatever letter they had reached being added to the list.

With your first letter chosen, play can commence. On "go" everyone has to write down a single answer to each category beginning with the chosen letter. The first person to complete all five shouts "Stop the bus" and everyone puts down their pencils and scores are totted up.

You get a point for every word you write down that correctly fits the category, but you also get an extra point if no-one else has gone for that same answer.

Now you pick another letter, add it to the next row and you're off again until all five rounds have been played and whoever has the most points is declared the winner. Unless you're on a bus, in which case, you should play until the bus driver asks you to leave.

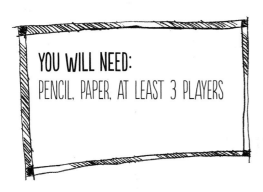

YOU WILL NEED:
PENCIL, PAPER, AT LEAST 3 PLAYERS

Tip: If you have a timer, you could play each round for a minute instead of waiting for someone to finish.

Example game

	Countries	Things that are green	Fruit	Clothes	Girls' names
A	Australia		Apple	Anorak	Abigail
B	Bulgaria	Bogeys	Banana	Bobblehat	Bethany
C	Canada	Cucumber	Cherry	Cap	Chloe
D	Denmark	Dad's jumper		Dungarees	Daphne
E	Ethiopia	Elves			Emma

STOP THE BUS!!

Make matchbox pets

These are perfect pets – small enough to put in your pocket, quiet enough not to upset the neighbours, very good at responding to both "sit" and "stay" commands and, best of all, absolutely no poo to clean up.

For starters you need to find a stone that will fit comfortably in your matchbox – have a look around outside and remember, you can make lots of different pets so don't feel you have to choose just one.

When your stone is clean and dry you can start creating your pet. Use paper or card to cut out different ears, feet or beaks – or anything else you want. Stick these on using PVA glue – just make sure you hold it in place until the glue is properly stuck. You can also use pieces of paper or card to form noses and eyes – hole-punched circles are useful for this – but equally you can simply draw on these details with a permanent marker.

The matchbox is going to be your pet's home so feel free to employ some interior design skills. You could use scraps of old felt or fabric to make a bed inside. Or why not draw around the base so you have the right size of paper, then decorate it as a "scene" to place your pet in?

Shoot a water cup race

What's more fun – beating your brother in a race… or squirting him in the face with water?

I know, choices, choices. It's difficult, right?

Well, this game makes it possible to do both. How good is that?

First you're going to need to set up your strings outside. You need one for each person playing and they must run between two points you can tie them to – something like a gate post or a handle. Ideally, your strings would end at the same point but they can start elsewhere – as long as the strings are roughly the same length so it's an equal race – about 5–8m (5½–8¾yds) long is ideal.

Now attach your string to the end point, but before you tie it to the starting point you need to prepare your cups. Place each one on a lump of sticky tack and then use a sharp pencil or pen to push through and make a hole right at a bottom edge. This needs to be big enough so it moves smoothly along the string, so test it and enlarge the hole if it gets stuck. When you're happy with them, thread one cup onto each string with the opening facing you before tying the end of the strings to the starting points. Just make sure the lines are nice and taut or the cups won't move along as well.

YOU WILL NEED:
STRING OR TWINE, PLASTIC CUPS, LUMP OF STICKY TACK, SHARP PENCIL OR BALLPOINT PEN, WATER PISTOLS

Now fill up your water pistols and on "go" everyone starts firing into their cups. If you're accurate and hit the bottom of the cup, the force of the water should start the cup moving along the string. As it moves, so can you, with the first person whose cup reaches the end of the line declared the winner.

And, of course, you can always try distracting your competitors by squirting water at them as well as in your cup. Just make sure you don't forget that, as much fun as this is, it's not actually the point of the game (at least not officially).

Tip: Use the same type of water pistol to make the race fair, or else make sure anyone with a more powerful gun has a longer string to race along.

Tip: If you hang herbs such as lavender and rosemary to the base you can have a beautifully scented dream catcher.

Weave a dream catcher

Do you have bad dreams? You know, like the one where you turn up for school wearing your underwear only to find you have a 10-hour exam you have forgotten to revise for? It's okay. Breathe. It was just a dream!

Still, it's good to know you're not alone. In fact, Native American tribes even had a solution to this. They made dream catchers that would trap bad dreams in their webs at night, only allowing the good ones to slip through and comfort them. Not that I'm saying they work, but hey, if there's a chance you won't dream about going to school in just your pants it's probably worth a shot.

Begin by bending your twig into a circle – willow works well for this but you can also try young twigs from other trees and shrubs. To hold this frame in place wrap a little garden wire around the join and twist the ends together. Now tie on some twine and wrap it round and round the join until it is firmly in place, then make a loop at one end, tie a knot at its base and wrap more of the twine around the frame before tying off the end.

Now cut a long length of twine, about 1.5m (1¾yds) long, tie one end onto the top of your dream catcher and then loop the other one over the willow frame a little way along before passing the twine through the gap that this has made.

Do this again and again until you come back to the top of the frame. Now do the same "loop and pass through" but this time at a point halfway along the first twine section you created. Repeat this until you have gone right around the circle again, leaving you with a flower-like pattern. You can add more of these circles until you are happy with the look, then cut off your twine and tie it onto the end of the last circle.

Finally, use your twine to attach natural objects to the base of your dream catcher, such as feathers, pinecones, leaves, shells or anything you fancy. Or you could include some more "glitzy" additions like beads or strips of fabric. I would avoid pants though.

YOU WILL NEED:
BENDY TWIG, GARDEN WIRE, TWINE OR STRING, SCISSORS, NATURAL OBJECTS

Draw outdoor chalk games

If you fancy a new game, there's no need to go to the shops or spend your precious pocket money. Just grab a stick of chalk and you can conjure one up outside.

What about a version of hopscotch with added squares and different moves – more of a hop-skip-jump-and-touch-your-toes-scotch?

Or draw a series of circles with scores written in each one, with those nearer the centre having higher scores. Then all you need are three pebbles each and a line drawn to stand behind and you can take it in turns to try and hit the target.

And if you are after some adventure, how about grabbing dice and some friends for a human-sized game of snakes and ladders? Just draw a grid, numbering the squares as you go, before deciding where you'll put your helpful ladders (which you can climb to the top of if you land on the bottom rung) and tricky snakes (which you will have to slide down if you land on their head).

Oh, and remember these are just drawn in chalk – no need to raid the tool shed or your local zoo.

YOU WILL NEED:
CHALK, DRIVE, PATHWAY OR PLAYGROUND, PEBBLES OR DICE, 2 OR MORE PLAYERS

Tip: Use different coloured chalks to make your games look even more artistic and exciting.

Bowl outdoors

Ever wondered what it's like to knock things over and not be yelled at? Well then it's time to try some outdoor 10-pin bowling.

This will need a bit of planning because you are going to need a lot of tin cans. But if you nag your parents, go through the recycling bin or maybe even ask your neighbours, you should be able to find the 10 you need without too much trouble.

Once a grown-up has checked there are no sharp edges on the tin cans and you have made sure they're clean, take your cans outside and find a nice flat piece of hard ground. Set them up in four rows – one at the front, two behind, three after this and a line of four to finish – so they form a triangle shape.

Now draw around each one in chalk and then add another line a little distance away – this is where the bowler has to stand.

Each player gets two tennis balls and must roll each one, trying to knock down as many cans altogether as they can. After each person's two rolls, replace the cans in their chalk position ready for the next player.

If anyone knocks down all 10 in their go, the cans are put back up and they also get a bonus throw – and get to do an annoyingly smug victory dance.

Decide how many rounds you are playing and the winner is whoever gets the most points in total. Oh, and if you have younger players who struggle to hit the cans you can move the bowling line nearer for them, let them use a bigger ball or even use old bricks or a pair of brooms to add "sides" to the bowling lane.

Tip: You can use old plastic bottles, partly filled with water, instead of cans – but as they are harder to knock over you will need to use a football to roll at them.

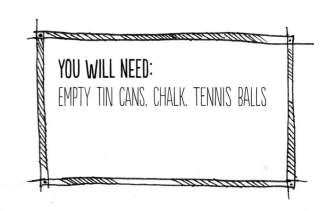

YOU WILL NEED:
EMPTY TIN CANS, CHALK, TENNIS BALLS

Lay out a stick house

I know a stick house didn't end well for the second little pig. But don't worry, because this one is already flattened, so what harm can a huffing, puffing wolf really do?

You can use any outdoor space you can find – a lawn, a patio, it doesn't really matter as long as it's big enough for the home you decide to create.

If you want, you can sketch out your ideas on paper first – deciding what rooms you want to have (bedrooms? bathrooms? kitchen? indoor gym? games room?) and where they sit inside your home. Or you can just start building and see where it goes.

Use the sticks or canes to mark out your walls. You can leave gaps for doors or smaller sections of sticks that you can "open" and "close" behind you.

This part can take some time. Especially if there is more than one of you making such crucial decisions as "Is there room in my bedroom for a 10-person sleepover because if not, that's a deal breaker?" and "Where is my walk-in wardrobe going to go?"

Of course, getting the layout right is only the first step. The fun really starts when you begin to furnish the place. Just remember, before you cart half the contents of your actual home outside, you might want to get the okay from a grown-up.

Getting a blanket or sleeping bag can make your bedroom a little cosier, and a few chairs or a beanbag will give you somewhere to sit, but equally you can be a little less traditional. How about a paddling pool in the living room, or a front door that can only be accessed via a slide? Or maybe a hallway that is also a crawl tunnel? Before you know it, architects around the country will be looking to you and your brilliant home for inspiration. Then again…

YOU WILL NEED:
OUTSIDE SPACE, PAPER AND PENCIL (OPTIONAL), STICKS OR BAMBOO CANES, FURNISHINGS

Tip: You can push bamboo canes into soft ground or into soil in pots to create uprights for your doorframes.

Try tape resist art

YOU WILL NEED:
MASKING OR PAINTERS' TAPE, PAPER OR CARD, SCISSORS, PAINT, PAINTBRUSHES

Have you ever found it hard to "colour inside the lines"? Well this is the art for you. Forget colouring inside the lines – you can paint where you want because you own these lines!

First of all you need to decide what to make with your art. Now your lines are created from tape so there are a lot of straight edges but there's nothing to stop you cutting some curvy tape too. Then again, that's more effort and if you couldn't be bothered to keep inside the lines in the first place, well…

Cut and stick the tape as you want onto your card or paper, but just make sure you only gently smooth it on because you're going to need to take it off again very shortly.

When you're happy with your tape masterpiece, you can begin painting on your colours. If you've made sections with your tape pieces you could paint these with different colours but equally a mix of different colours, maybe even blending into each other, can also look really effective.

And when your paint is dry, you get to see the magic. Carefully lift up the edge of a piece of tape and slowly – very slowly – start to peel it off. If you rush this you may pull the paper off too so it's worth taking your time. What you will be left with is perfectly sharp lines in a truly dramatic work of art. See – it's not so hard after all.

Tip: For a longer lasting work of art, you can use acrylic paint on canvas.

Make tin can organizers

Tin cans are really too good to be used for something as boring as storing baked beans or tomatoes. If you want to give them an exciting new lease of life you can decorate them to make perfect organizers.

Before you begin, get a grown-up to check your tin cans have no sharp edges. Once that's done, for a super simple and quick makeover all you need to do is measure the height of your tin from just below its metal rim to the base. Now use the ruler and a pencil and mark this out on some paper, card or even fabric.

To work out how long you need to make the covering, use a piece of string to measure around the can and then lay this out along your paper, card or fabric to show you where to draw the end line. Just make sure you allow an extra centimetre (½in) or so for overlap. When this rectangular shape is marked, cut it out and then paste your tin with PVA glue before carefully wrapping your covering around. Add a little extra glue at the point of overlap to make sure it sticks down.

If you have a large tin, such as an old, clean paint can, this can be decorated in the same way to make the perfect centre piece. You can then

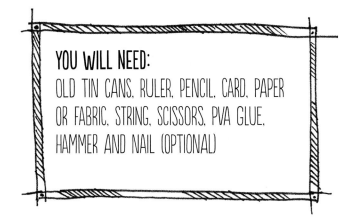

YOU WILL NEED:
OLD TIN CANS, RULER, PENCIL, CARD, PAPER OR FABRIC, STRING, SCISSORS, PVA GLUE, HAMMER AND NAIL (OPTIONAL)

group the small tins around the edge to end up with a multi-section organizer that you can keep anything in. But maybe not baked beans.

Tip: If you ask a grown-up to use a hammer and nail to carefully knock several holes in the bottom of your cans, you can also use these as pretty planters for your windowsill

Play spoons

This game involves very little skill and is super easy to pick up, so the good news is grown-ups might even be able to play it too.

Begin by sitting around a table or on the floor and placing spoons in the middle: one less than the number of people playing.

Next, the dealer gives everyone, including themselves, four cards, face down, and keeps the remaining pack close at hand. Now they pick a card from the main pack and quickly decide whether to keep this or pass it face down to the person on their left. As soon as they've done this they pick up the next card from the deck and

again decide either to keep or pass on. At the same time the person on their left is doing the same thing and passing a card, face down to the person on their left. The only exception is the person on the dealer's right, who also picks up a card from their neighbour but puts the card they decide to pass on face up on a discard pile.

The aim is to collect four of a kind – such as four sixes or four aces. The first person who manages this takes a spoon from the centre. And as soon as they make their move, everyone tries to do the same, grabbing a spoon before they have all gone.

The one person who fails to get a spoon in time is out, another spoon is removed and a new round begins, this time with the person to the dealer's left taking over dealing duties. And you keep going until there is just one person left holding a spoon in victory.

Alternatively, if you want to keep players in for longer, each time a player loses they take a letter from S-P-O-O-N. When they spell out the whole word, they are out.

And if you run out of draw cards, you just have to reshuffle the discard pile and use this.

Make a washer pendant

YOU WILL NEED:
METAL WASHER, GREASEPROOF PAPER OR OLD PLASTIC SHEET, NAIL VARNISH, STICKY TAPE, HAIR PIN, TOOTHPICK, OLD CHAIN, LEATHER STRAP OR STRING

You might not expect the parts of a kitchen tap or toilet to make great jewellery, but I'm here to tell you they really do. I'm not suggesting you wear a toilet seat as a headpiece or use tap spouts as earrings, but a metal washer does make the perfect pendant.

Of course, you had better not take the actual washer from the tap or toilet – that will be messy – but grown-ups often have spare ones lying around so ask if you can upcycle one of these.

Place your washer on a sheet of greaseproof paper or old plastic sheet before deciding which nail varnish colours to use and in what way.

You could paint on a base coat of one colour and then leave it to dry. If you want to make a dramatic two-tone look, mask one side with sticky tape and paint over the other with a second colour. When this has dried, remove the tape to reveal a perfectly crisp line.

For a dotty look, dip the rounded end of a hair pin into the nail varnish and touch it to the washer for a mini circle.

And if you love a marbled look, add a base colour and while it's still wet, drip other colours of nail varnish on top. Now use the end of a toothpick to swirl the colours together until you are happy with the look.

When the washer has dried, turn it over and decorate the other side. Finally, when this has also set, get your chain, string or leather strap and tie on the pendant using the lark's head knot (see page 61).

Tip: You can add a smaller washer on top of a larger one for a double pendant.

Make balloon creatures

When you blow up a balloon, who knows where it will end? Yes, you're right – possibly in a BANG! which is quite scary, but also it could end with a flamingo, or an alien or maybe even a dinosaur. Because that's the thing with balloons, they are perfect for creating all sorts of fantastic creatures – it just requires a bit of imagination.

First you'll need to blow up a balloon. If you stretch it out a few times first, it's easier to inflate, or you can use a balloon pump… or a grown-up (they're quite handy for these things), making sure you tie it at the end (the balloon, not the grown-up).

Now you'll need to add some details with a permanent pen – or, if you are a bit nervous, use a whiteboard/dry erase marker and then you'll be able to rub off any mistakes with a damp, soapy cloth or wet wipe.

You can make an alien face, or a ghost very easily with just a black pen, but it's also possible to add some simple shapes to make ears, arms, legs, tails – or anything really. These are best cut from paper or card and then the end connected to the balloon with some sticky tape. If you want to stick on perhaps a nose or mouth flat to the balloon, use a glue stick or double-sided sticky tape.

Just remember, be very gentle when you're adding your details, otherwise it will all end very quickly, and loudly!

Tip: Stick a piece of white cotton to the balloon and use this to dangle your creation invisibly.

YOU WILL NEED:
BALLOON, PERMANENT
MARKER OR
WHITEBOARD/DRY ERASE
MARKER, PAPER OR CARD,
SCISSORS, STICKY TAPE,
GLUE STICK OR DOUBLE-
SIDED STICKY TAPE,
COTTON (OPTIONAL)

Create an autumn leaf picture frame

Autumn leaves are brilliant for kicking about – but they can also make a fabulous picture frame. Maybe one that can frame a picture of you… kicking autumn leaves.

To begin, take a bowl or small plate and draw around it in the centre of your paper plate. If you bend the plate gently over and snip with some scissors you will have an opening that you can then use to cut out the circle to make the centre of your frame.

Now use a slightly larger plate or bowl to create another circle on some card – this will be the back of your picture frame.

To hold the two pieces together, make three retainers from the card. These should be about 2cm (¾in) wide and 3cm (1¼in) long, but you won't see them so it doesn't matter if they're not perfectly precise.

Make a hole in the bottom of the retainers by pushing a sharp pencil through them into a lump of sticky tack beneath. Now draw around your larger circle on the back of the plate so you can see where the back of the picture frame will sit and then push the pencil through again to make matching holes for your retainers just outside this circle in three evenly spaced spots.

Push the split pins through each retainer and the frame from the back of the frame and open them at the front. Make another two holes at the top of the frame and thread through some string, tying the ends together to make a hook.

To decorate, use PVA glue to stick on your autumn leaves so they cover up all the paper plate ring. Then, to make sure they stick down well, sandwich the frame between two large plates, put some weight such as heavy books on top, and leave it for about an hour to dry.

Tip: You can also use pressed flowers to decorate a paper plate frame for a more summery look.

In the meantime, take your card circle that forms the back of the frame and either draw on this to make a picture for the frame, or simply draw around the circle on a picture you already have (like the one of you kicking the autumn leaves perhaps), cut out the circle and stick it onto the card.

Finally, when the frame has dried, place the picture in the frame and twist the retainers around to hold it in place.

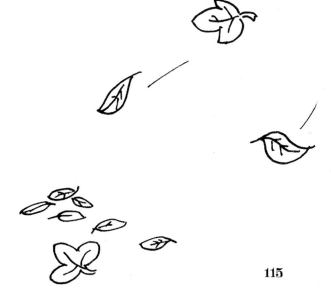

Freeze some hands

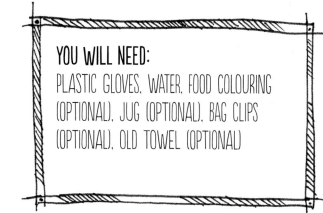

The biggest difficulty with this project is trying not to break off too many fingers.

Oh dear. You've gone a little pale. Maybe I should have explained that you're not freezing your own hands here. Sorry about that.

Yes, the frozen hands are actually created by the plastic gloves. First of all you need to fill your glove with water. You can do this either straight from the tap or, if you want to add a bit of colour, mix your water with a few drops of food colouring in a jug and then pour it in.

Make sure you leave some space at the end of the glove to close it off. It's easiest to do this using bag clips, but if you haven't got any, you can tie a knot in the end as though it were a balloon (or get a grown-up to help if this proves too tricky).

Now you need to lay the filled glove in the freezer – or if it's a very cold winter's day you could leave it outside overnight. Just make sure that the fingers are properly spaced out or it will be trickier to take the glove off afterwards.

Next morning you can take the frozen hand and run it under a cold tap for a few seconds. Now it's time to remove the glove. It's easiest to do this with the hand lying on an old towel to cushion it.

Start carefully by taking off the clip and rolling back the bottom of the glove slowly and carefully. If you do break off the odd finger, don't panic. When you're done, stand the hand upright and put the fingers back in place. The cold of the ice will refreeze the melting water at the edge and should reattach the finger in a couple of minutes.

The finished hands are great in winter to place around the garden as ice sculptures, or emerging from a snow pile if you want to give someone a scare. In summer they make brilliant ice blocks that can be placed in bowls to keep drinks cool.

YOU WILL NEED:
STRING, TWINE
OR STRONG THREAD,
A STRAW, BALLOON,
BINDER CLIP
(OPTIONAL), STICKY
TAPE

Launch a balloon rocket

First, tie the end of your string to a handle, a piece of furniture – or if you're outside, perhaps a tree trunk or fence post. Unravel as much length as you would like but probably at least 5m (5½yds) to give the rocket space to travel.

Now thread the other end of your string through the straw and lay this carefully on the floor.

Blow up the balloon as much as you can and then either get a friend to hold the end tight or use a binder clip to stop the air escaping.

You need to attach the balloon to the straw with a couple of pieces of sticky tape and, most importantly, so the end of the balloon is facing you.

Finally, pull the string tight in one hand and let go of the clip with the other and you have lift off! The balloon should zoom along the string to the end of the line as fast as… well, a balloon rocket.

Tip: If you set up two lines you can race balloons with a friend.

Make a climbing mouse

Hickory, dickory dock, the mouse ran up the clock. Why? We've no idea. Mice are just like that, I guess.

Still, if you wish to create this slightly inexplicable mouse adventure, it's easy enough to do with a simple piece of paper.

Begin by taking the long side of your sheet and folding it over about a third of the way across. Line up the top and bottom edges to make sure they're straight and then press down the fold.

Next cut along this folded line so you are left with a long strip (diagram 1). Fold it over top to bottom and then side to side. Now undo the last fold (diagram 2) and then bend down each of the top corners to meet the middle line, firmly press down these folds (diagram 3).

Bend back the upper right-hand fold then squash the top flat so you have formed a triangle above the rectangle beneath (diagrams 4–5). Turn over your paper and do the same thing again.

Carefully cut off the top of your triangle (diagram 6) and use pens or pencils to decorate this very triangular mouse. Afterwards you can decorate your grandfather clock.

Finally, slip your mouse between the two sides of your clock (diagram 7) which you then take hold of before moving them up and down (diagram 8). Magically your mouse should start to climb up that clock. I've still no idea why though.

OOPS!

Making a clock and mouse

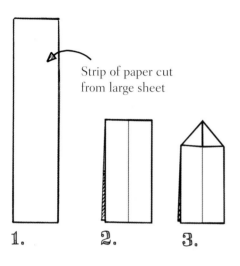

Strip of paper cut from large sheet

1.

2.

3.

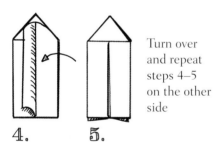

4.

5.

Turn over and repeat steps 4–5 on the other side

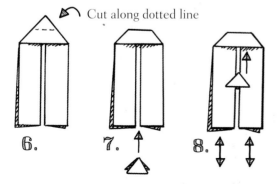

Cut along dotted line

6.

7.

8.

Tip: If you are less interested in mice you could choose to go for a flying superhero and a skyscraper, or anything else you fancy.

Play consequences

Let's be clear – this is a very silly game. Yes, I thought you'd like that. It's also best played with plenty of people because silliness like this deserves to be shared.

Every player starts with a sheet or wide strip of paper. Now everybody has to write down the first sort of word or phrase before folding the top of the paper over so what they have written cannot be seen. Then everyone passes the paper to the person on their left and everyone adds the next thing on the list.

You can use the ideas below or add or alter this to make your own version of the game.

Person A
Person B
Where they met
What they went there for
What person A wore
What person B wore
What A said to B
What B said to A
The consequence
What the world said

Tip: You can play picture consequences where you take it in turn to draw the head, then body, then legs, then feet.

When the last item has been added, you pass on the piece of paper for the last time and everyone takes it in turn to unroll the paper and read what has been written. Of course, as nobody had a clue what anyone else had said, this is usually some very silly (but entertaining) nonsense, such as:

Granny met the Invisible Man at the circus. They went there to learn the ancient art of hula hooping. She wore a space suit. He wore a tiara. She said: "I've never looked my best in a leotard." He said: "Sorry, that smell is me." The consequence was the creation of a new country called Bogeytown. The world said: "We all knew that would happen."

As I say, very, very silly.

YOU WILL NEED:
PAPER, PENCILS OR PENS,
AT LEAST 3 PLAYERS

Try cup weaving

We really should rename disposable plastic cups. "Reusable cups" would be better. Or how about calling them "the start of a really lovely woven container"? Bit long? You may have a point.

But it is accurate, because a simple plastic cup can be turned into something rather beautiful with the help of a little wool. First, you need to make nine slits up the side of the cup to form nine equal sections – you can use the circle opposite to help. Just hold your cup upside down over it and mark the nine segments. Now, remove your cup and, at each marked point, use scissors to carefully cut a slit all the way down the side.

Next, tie the end of your wool around one of the segments, so the ends are hidden inside the cup. Slip another cup inside the first to help give it strength and shape and begin taking your wool in and out of the segments as you go round and round the cup. As you weave, use your fingers to push down the pieces of wool so you can't see any gaps.

When you want to change colour, simply cut the end of your first piece of wool and tie the second one on. Try to do this so the tied ends finish up inside the cup again – that way the outside always looks neat.

When you reach the top of the cup, cut the end of the wool, leaving a little extra. Now take out the inside cup so you can see the wool underneath

and pass the cut end under the piece of wool just in front of it inside the cup, and tie it on.

If your cup has a clear inside, you can try to trim the ends of the tied sections so they don't show before slipping the cup back in. If it's not see-through, you can skip this step. Either way, this second cup will make the whole thing sturdier and protect the wool from anything you may store inside it.

To finish off, you can use some lengths of wool to make decorative plaits. If the wool is very thin, use two strands per plait section (six in total) to make a chunkier edging. Keep checking the length needed as you go and then tie it off and trim the ends when it's long enough. You can attach it using PVA glue.

YOU WILL NEED:
2 DISPOSABLE PLASTIC CUPS, PEN, SCISSORS, WOOL, PVA GLUE, CLOTHES PEGS (OPTIONAL)

Tip: Use clothes pegs to hold the top plait in place as the glue dries.

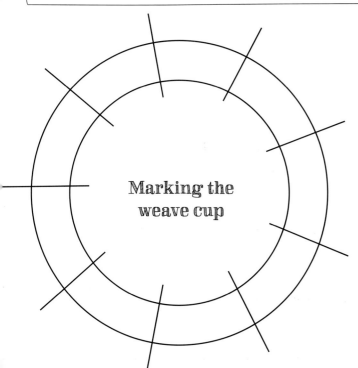

Marking the weave cup

Make a mini scarecrow

The trouble with a full-size scarecrow is that it's a bit too… scary. After all, it's supposed to put off birds from eating your crops, not give children nightmares. Instead, how about making a smaller version? It might still bother the odd crow, but at least you'll sleep at night.

First, lay the bamboo cane across the broom handle about a third of the way down to form a cross shape. Tie on the twine using a clove hitch knot (see page 61) and then wrap the twine around the join lots of times in a figure of eight pattern before tying the ends together tightly to hold it in place.

You'll need some clothes to dress your mini scarecrow in. If you have a younger brother or sister you may want to see if there are any outfits that they have grown out of or else you can look in charity shops.

Dress your cross shape in the old T-shirt and put the pair of dungarees over the top. You will need to cut a hole at the top of the legs to push the broom handle through. Using twine, tie the ends of the sleeves and trousers, leaving a very small gap so you can add some straw later.

Now use scrunched-up newspaper or old plastic bags inserted through the neck of the T-shirt and the top of the dungarees to fill out the body of your scarecrow. To make feet, hands and neck, add a handful of straw into each of the openings.

You now need to push the bottom of the broom handle into the ground wherever you want your scarecrow to stand. If this is a little tough, maybe find a grown-up to help (see, they can be useful like that sometimes).

Finally, finish off by placing your plant pot upside down on top of the broomstick as a head and topping with an old hat… because nothing says "scary" to birds more than a pint-sized, dungaree-wearing, plant pot-headed figure in a cute hat.

YOU WILL NEED:
THICK BAMBOO CANE ABOUT 60CM (24IN) LONG, OLD BROOM
HANDLE, TWINE OR STRING, LONG-SLEEVED CHILD'S T-SHIRT,
CHILD'S DUNGAREES, SCRUNCHED-UP NEWSPAPERS OR OLD
PLASTIC BAGS, STRAW, PLANT POT, OLD HAT

Tip: You can draw a
face onto the plant pot
with acrylic paint – and
maybe add a jaunty
neckerchief.

Try balloon printing

You can use normal balloons for this art project but filled water balloons are even better because they're heavier, making them print more easily, and squishier, making them nicer to hold. Just remember, they're also a lot... well, wetter – so be careful!

First, fill your balloon with water (or blow it up if you're using an ordinary balloon) and tie it off. Make sure it's the right size for the prints you want to make and that it's dry.

Now protect your table with old newspapers and then take your bowl and add your main paint colour before drizzling swirls of two or three more contrasting colours on top.

Finally, take hold of the top of the balloon, dip it into the paint and then begin to print circles on your paper.

You can print several times without redipping your balloon and each one should give a magical "tie dye" effect with the different colours splaying into each other in amazing patterns.

Just remember, don't press too hard or your balloon could burst and you may find that your parents are less keen on "water colours" when they drip all over the floor.

Tip: Use different-sized balloons or alternative paint colour combinations to make a more complex picture.

Compete in no-hands eating

"Have you washed your hands?"

"Let me see your fingernails."

"Did you actually use any soap?"

Yes, parents are a wee bit obsessed when it comes to clean hands and eating. Do you know what will solve this? That's right – don't use your hands at all.

Of course, there's nothing to stop you doing this at every meal – well, except your parents' utter horror as you dunk your head into your cereal bowl. But it's probably best to limit it to something slightly less messy – but incredibly delicious – like doughnuts.

And best of all, doughnuts are perfect for dangling, making this even more fun.

You'll need something to hang them from. A washing line is perfect or you can tie a string between two points – inside or outside, it's up to you (and how fussy your parents are about crumbs).

Now simply thread some more string through the hole in the doughnut and then tie this onto the line so it dangles at about head height. If you hang several it means you can invite your mucky-handed friends to join in too.

On "go", the aim of the game is simple: just try to eat your doughnut as quickly as possible, without letting it fall off the line. It's not easy – but hey, practice makes perfect!

Tip: For a healthier version, ask an adult to core and slice an apple to hang from the string.

YOU WILL NEED:
STRING, DOUGHNUTS

Make a tape town

So what would happen if you put kids in charge of town planning? I know – let's find out!

The good news is this experiment won't involve expensive diggers and bulldozers, just a roll of masking tape.

This sort of tape is very easy to lift off carpets and floors, even sofas and walls, so you can lay out your town anyway you wish, and just as easily change your mind.

A road system is a good starting point. You could make single lanes with thick masking tape or use two lines with some central markings to create dual lanes. And then, of course, there is no reason you can't add bigger, wider motorway sections, roundabouts and car parks.

And why limit yourself to cars? If you have different toys like planes, trains and small figures you could add an airport runway, train tracks and pedestrian crossings.

In the spaces in between, you can include buildings made out of cardboard boxes: houses, hospitals, shops, even… schools.

But why stop there? Let your imagination run riot! A giant open air swimming pool could be made out of shiny foil, a hillside out of cushions and a blanket, and a helicopter pad out of a giant masking tape "H" positioned so you can land right outside the ice cream parlour. Now there's an idea…

Tip: You can use different coloured tapes for a brighter looking town.

Dig a beach pool

YOU WILL NEED:
A BEACH, OLD SHOWER CURTAIN OR LARGE PIECE OF PLASTIC SHEET, BUCKET AND SPADE

If you want to upgrade your next beach visit, it's a good idea to take along an old shower curtain. Although this might not sound like the height of glamour, it is the perfect way to create your own private beach pool.

First decide on the right spot. You'll be doing some digging so make sure you choose soft sand to make this easier and try to find somewhere that the seawater won't cover when the tide comes in.

Now begin to dig your hole. It should be about half the size of your shower curtain or piece of plastic. If you keep stopping and laying this over the hole as you work, you can check you're on track. The important thing is that the plastic will line the bottom and sides but still have a little extra left to line around the top.

When you're happy with the shape of your hole, lay the shower curtain or plastic sheet in it and then you can start filling the pool with buckets of water collected from the sea.

Once you have put in enough water to hold down the base of the shower curtain or plastic sheet, you need to tidy up the edges around the top. You can either simply cover these with more sand or dig a small slit trench and push in the edges. If you like, you can decorate the edges with pebbles or shells.

Finally, when your pool is filled, it's time to sit back and relax in it. And no, it's not big enough to swim in, but after all that work who needs any more exercise? And of course you need to save enough energy to empty it out and fold up your shower curtain or plastic sheet to take it home with you when it's time to go – all ready to create your next luxury beach pool.

Tip: Create a luxury feel by adding a parasol for shade and perhaps a tray by the side to hold your drink and snacks.

Rustle up nachos

Here's a useful tip: rather than asking "Can I eat a bag of tortilla chips?" try saying "Shall I rustle us up some tasty nachos?" To grown-ups you will appear to be a culinary wizard generously catering for your family, but the end result will still involve you eating a tasty mountain of tortilla chips, so it's the perfect result all round.

Oh, and on top of all that, it requires almost no effort.

Just take your serving dish and spread tortilla chips across the base. Now open the jar of salsa and shake the salsa over the top of the crisp base so it's evenly spread. Next sprinkle on the cheese before finally using your craft scissors to snip up your spring onion all over the top.

And if you like a bit of Mexican heat to your nachos, you could add a pinch or two of chilli flakes.

If you prefer your cheese melted and your chips and salsa warmed, you can finish your nachos off in the microwave. Just give it 20 seconds at a time and keep an eye on it. When the cheese melts, it's done. Just be sure to use oven gloves or ask a grown-up to help take the nachos out, as the dish may be hot.

Tip: You can serve this with soured cream or guacamole for extra dipping options.

Hold wacky relay races

There is, of course, nothing to stop you holding "incredibly sensible relay races", but that sounds much less fun.

Instead, choose one or more of these ideas – it's a great way to liven up a party, or *especially* a family get together. After all, what's more fun than watching your granny accidentally tipping water over her head or your uncle getting stuck in a hula hoop? Exactly!

Water bucket relay

Two teams sit cross-legged in a line, a full bucket at the front and an empty one at the back. The person at the front takes a plastic cup and fills it from the full bucket before passing it over their head to the person behind. This keeps going until the last person has to pour it backward over their head into the bucket at the back.

The game continues until a bucket at the front is empty but the winning team is actually the one with the most water in their finish bucket at this point – rather than over each other's heads.

Partner ball relay

Working in pairs, players have to transport a ball held between their backs to the finish line. The bigger the ball, the easier this is. If you only have smaller ones such as tennis balls, try doing it forehead to forehead instead.

Tunnel relay

Teams stand in a line, legs apart, and on "go" the person at the back starts crawling through everyone's legs. At the end, they run around to tag the next person at the back and then return to the front with their own legs apart. The first team to get everyone to complete it has won (and probably has slightly grubby knees).

Hula hoop relay

Two teams stand in a line and hold hands. On "go" the end person picks up a hula hoop and without letting go of hands each team has to pass it from one end of their line to the other. Bigger hoops are easier – and are less likely to trap your uncle – but where's the fun in that?

Tip: Try using a balloon instead of a ball for a partner balloon relay that is ideal for playing inside.

YOU WILL NEED:
BUCKETS AND PLASTIC CUPS, WATER, BALLS, HULA HOOPS, LOTS OF PEOPLE

Mix memory sand

Playing with sand is fun – we can all agree on that. But here's what you might not know: it can be even better. Yes – amazing but true!

And what's more, to create this "new-and-improved" magical memory sand you only need three simple added ingredients – cornflour, water and washing-up liquid.

Although brilliant, this sand can still be a little messy, so to prevent parents doing that "crossing-arms-and pulling a-frowny-face" move, you are best making this in a large plastic container. If you can find one with a lid, that's even better, as you can then store your sand afterwards, ready to use another day.

First of all, measure out six cups of play sand into your container followed by a cup and a half of cornflour before mixing these two together really well with your hands. Now add two teaspoons (or two big squirts) of washing up liquid to your cup, which you should then fill to around three quarters full with water. Use your fingers or a teaspoon to stir these two together thoroughly before pouring it on top of your sand.

Finally, dig in with your hands and squish, squelch and swirl all these ingredients to form your mouldable, magic memory sand.

You can just play with the sand as it is, or bring in moulds, cookie cutters and containers to create all sorts of shapes. If it feels too wet, don't worry, it will dry out as you play with it. And if it dries too much? Just add more water.

When you're finished you can put on the lid and pack it away, and if you want to play with it again, all you need to do is add water and washing-up liquid again and your memory sand is back in business.

Make a mini lantern garland

You can make larger versions of these lanterns but smaller, as we all know, is cuter (unless we're referring to a little brother or sister when they are being particular annoying).

Take your first piece of card and measure and cut four 2cm (¾in) wide strips from the shorter side. Now fold the card in half so the shorter sides meet, then unfold and cut along the crease to make two rectangles.

Do exactly the same with the second piece of card in the contrasting colour.

Now take one of the rectangles, fold it in half lengthways and then measure a 2cm (¾in) strip at the bottom. Mark a series of 1.5cm (⅔in) lines all the way along from the folded centre down to meet the bottom strip with the last line drawn in to the bottom of the card (see diagram). Carefully cut along these lines to form one small strip of card and then another larger section with slits all along.

Now to save you rubbing out all the pencil marks, open up your card and fold it over in the other direction so the marks are now all on the inside. Next add glue to the outside edge and overlap the strips at both ends.

To get the two-tone effect, add a strip cut from the contrasting card to the top and bottom of your lantern. Do the same with the other half of the card and then the two rectangles from the contrasting card, giving you four lanterns all together. And, of course, if you use two more sheets of card, you can make eight.

Finally, glue or staple the small strip of card you cut earlier to the inside top edge of the lantern to form a handle. Now simply thread your lantern handles onto your ribbon, alternating the colours of the lanterns as you go. If you loop the ribbon through each handle twice, you will stop the handles sliding around.

You can string your lanterns up as they are, or even thread a few fairy lights along the string and down into each lantern to make them into a light feature.

Tip: You can also make single lanterns to stand on their own. These look lovely with an electric tealight inside.

Making a lantern

1.

2cm (¾in)

Cut 4 strips

2.

Fold and cut

3.

Fold

4. cut down all slits ⌐ Cut off last strip

2cm (¾in) 1.5cm (²⁄₃in)

Cut out paper snowflakes

These are perfect winter decorations. In fact, they're perfect decorations full stop, so maybe we need to stop calling them "snowflakes" and instead call them "all-year-round-whatever-the-weather flakes". That should cover it.

Begin by drawing circles on your piece of paper, fitting them as close to each other as possible so you don't waste space. Next, you need to cut them out with your scissors. If you're very careful, you can lay two or three sheets of paper on top of each other and create more than one circle at a time.

When you have a circle, fold it in half, then half again, and half one more time.

Now it's time to get creative. Begin snipping shapes out of the sides of your folded paper, and also from its top and point. You can follow some of the ideas on the opposite page, but it's even more fun to come up with your own designs. You can draw lines on to follow or simply cut where you like.

When you think you've snipped enough, begin to unfold your creation, taking care not to rush it or you may rip the paper.

If you don't think there's enough detail, you can refold and carry on snipping. However, if it is, as you suspect, already a work of genius, then unfold it and either use sticky tack to attach it to a cupboard door, mirror or window, or sticky tape some cotton to it and dangle it from somewhere it can be seen and admired by all.

Tip: Use different coloured paper for a brighter all-year-round-flake.

Paper snowflake ideas

Weave stick spider webs

YOU WILL NEED:
3 STICKS, THIN GARDEN WIRE, WOOL, SCISSORS

It's time to take on the spiders at their own game. Okay, so you might not be able to make your own silk thread, or weave something that can trap flies, but you might just beat them on the clock. Yes, it takes a spider an hour to weave a web, so, on your marks, get set… go!

Start with three sticks. These should be roughly the same size, the same length and not too smooth. Your web will need something to catch on, so knobbly sticks are a definite plus.

Lay your three sticks out so they cross in the middle and are evenly spaced like spokes in a wheel. You could try tying these together with string or twine, but it's a lot easier to use a length of thin garden wire bent and twisted around and between the sticks again and again until the shape is held very firmly in place.

Now take your wool. You can start by using this to go over the wire at the centre to cover it up. When you are happy with the look, cut the end of the wool and tie the two ends together, trimming off the ends neatly.

Now tie the end of the wool to one of the twigs, quite near the centre before taking the wool around and around the spokes. The wool should form a spiral as you wrap it around each spoke in turn, pulling it nice and tight each time. Eventually, when your wool web has reached near the end of your twigs, tie it securely, but leave a long end of wool. You can use this to hang your web up somewhere.

And now all that's left to do is check the clock, make sure you've beaten the spider's record and then celebrate with some lovely juicy flies.*

*(Optional.)

Tip: If you don't have wool, you could use string or twine instead.

Hold a thumb war

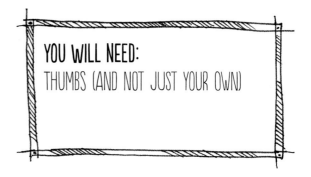

YOU WILL NEED:
THUMBS (AND NOT JUST YOUR OWN)

Let's be clear, declaring a war is generally a Very Bad Thing. But rather than massing forces on enemy lines, invading foreign lands or risking bloodshed, we're just talking about some good-natured digit wrestling, so I think we're okay. Unless, of course, you haven't cut your nails for months, in which case bloodshed could be a distinct possibility.

Right, have you trimmed your nails now? Good. We're safe to start.

First, you need to stand or sit opposite your opponent and hook the four fingers of your right (or left) hands together and hold them tightly. Now you need to solemnly bow your thumbs toward each other (who said wars can't be polite?) before chanting "One, two, three four, I declare a thumb-a-war!" and letting battle commence.

The aim is to pin down your opponent's thumb long enough to say "One, two, three four, I win thumb-a-war!"

And that's it.

Oh, yes, except for the little matter of rules. Well, you'll be delighted to hear there are very few, but if you are a stickler for such things, it's worth noting that you should keep elbows on the table (if you're even sitting at one). Oh, and inch-long nails sharpened to a point are a definite no-no.

Tip: If you want, you can play best of three or best of five rounds. You could even time rounds for no more than 60 seconds.

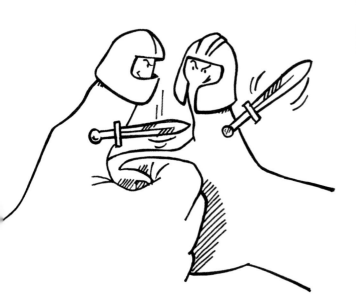

Create an outdoor race track

YOU WILL NEED:
SPADE, PVC PIPE, BRICKS, CHALK, TOY CARS

As this is a race track for toy cars, you could use a toy digger to construct it. Then again, if you want it built in an afternoon rather than a month, I'd stick to using a spade.

First, you'll need a spot to build on. A patch of soil is ideal as you can dig and shape the area. Just make sure you check with a grown-up first in case they have plans for that spot that don't involve fast-paced toy cars.

Now have a think about the shape of your track. Something that loops works well as cars can keep going round and round. You can also think about adding some areas of interest. One good idea is adding a mountainside tunnel. This can be made from a piece of PVC pipe. It doesn't need to be very long, but it should be wide enough for all your cars to fit through easily.

You can place your pipe on the ground and then mound soil over the top, and even add some stones near the entrances to disguise it. If it's set at a bit of an angle, you'll also find the cars shoot through on their own without you needing to push them (or worry about them getting stuck).

For the rest of the track you can use bricks. If you dig a trench and place your bricks in this they will sit level with the ground, or you can simply mound earth up against them. Bricks don't curve easily so you may find it easier to make very square turns for the cars. And if you want to make two lanes, simply use some chalk to draw these on.

Tip: If you want to keep the race track there permanently, you can grow plants around it for extra interest and use masonry paint for your road markings.

Fold a Chinese fan

Do you know the perfect thing to cool you down on a hot sunny day?

No. I wasn't thinking of a swimming pool. Have another go.

No. Not a cold drink full of ice either.

Oh come on. A FAN!

Yes, and unlike swimming pools and ice cold drinks, this will fit into your pocket so it's the perfect out-and-about cooler.

Begin by using your ruler and pencil to lightly mark a line 2cm (¾in) in on the shorter side of your paper. You can then use it as a guide to make your first fold and crease it down firmly. Now fold the paper in the opposite direction and carry on this "accordion folding" pattern until you reach the end of the sheet before doing the same with your other piece of paper.

Take your long folded sections and bend each one in half, being careful to line them up as precisely as you can. Next use glue to stick together the centre strips of each bent section and then the

two sections themselves (see diagram). Use clothes pegs to hold them in place while the glue dries or put a weight on top. Now attach together the folded ends of your fan shapes by wrapping sticky tape around the bottom 2cm (¾in).

Use the glue to stick together each pair of lollipop or craft sticks. Do this so one overlaps half of the other stick and weight them down or use clothes pegs to hold them in place until they're dry. Finally, glue the sticks onto either side of your fan so the sticks go up to, but not over, the taped section. When this is fully dry you can practise opening out your fan. When you close it again, use a small elastic band or hair band to hold the fan together.

Tip: For a fancy edge you can pre-cut your paper with decorative scissors or use a hole punch.

Making a fan

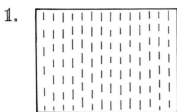

1.

2.

3.

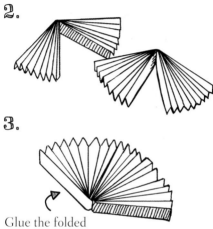

Glue the folded
sections together

4.

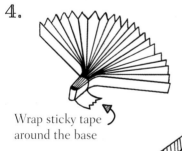

Wrap sticky tape
around the base

5.

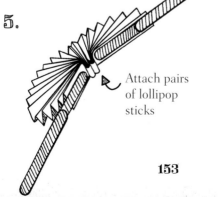

Attach pairs
of lollipop
sticks

153

Construct 3D stars

These 3D stars look so professional and impressive everyone will probably think you bought them. Which is outrageous after all that effort!

Actually, they're not even that difficult to make, but shhh… no need to let on.

You will need two matching squares of card. To make these take a sheet and fold one corner over to create a triangle and, making sure the edges line up, press the crease in firmly and then trim off the excess at the bottom. When you unfold the triangle you'll see you are left with a square.

Now fold each square corner to corner, unfold, and then edge to edge and unfold again. Use scissors to cut roughly halfway in on each straight horizontal and vertical crease (see diagram 1) and then fold in the flaps this makes to create triangle shapes lined up with the diagonal fold line (see diagram 2).

Glue the top of one triangle and place the other one over it to stick them together to form a 3D point. Now do the same for the other three and then do all this again with the other piece of paper or card.

Use a hole punch or a sharp pencil to make a hole at the flat underside of one of the points on one of your four-pointed stars, then thread it with wool or cotton.

Finally, place your two four-pointed shapes on top of each other, flat sides together, to make an eight-sided star. Mark where they overlap and then put a blob of PVA glue on these points before pressing the shapes back together.

Once it's dry, use your wool or thread to dangle your star where everyone can see and admire it.

YOU WILL NEED:
2 SHEETS OF A4 CARD, SCISSORS, GLUE STICK, HOLE PUNCH OR SHARP PENCIL, PVA GLUE, WOOL OR THREAD

Tip: If you don't have card you can also make these stars with paper.

Make a 3D star

Cut along dotted line

Cut along dotted line

Cut along dotted line

Cut along dotted line

1.

2.

Make snack art

Van Gogh's *Sunflowers*, Michelangelo's *David*, Monet's *Water Lilies*: all amazing artworks, but the real question is – could you eat them?

No! Exactly. Which is why snack art beats them all.

You need to begin by trying to decide what to create: maybe a favourite animal or cartoon character, a garden or a beach, a spaceship in outer space or a deep sea diver under the sea or something completely different!

Now comes the tricky part: how to make this from just snacks.

If you have cookie cutters you could use these to form some useful shapes from bread or sandwiches, or if you have smaller cutters, even from something like a cucumber or banana.

When you have some key pieces you can use, start placing them on a plate. It's easiest to use a plain plate so your design really stands out.

You may be able to use some small items whole like berries, dried fruit, mangetout, cherry tomatoes, orange segments or grapes. Others could be used grated (like carrot) or in long peel sections (like carrot and cucumber). If you do need anything sliced it might be easier to ask a grown-up to help – or perhaps to prepare them in advance. And if you are using things like apples and bananas, sprinkle them with some lemon juice as this will stop them turning brown.

You can create pictures on your own, but it's even more fun to make it a competition and then set up your own snack plate gallery. Just remember, the one rule of snack art is: you have to eat it all up afterwards!

YOU WILL NEED:
BREAD, SELECTION OF FRUIT AND VEGETABLES,
COOKIE CUTTERS, PEELER OR GRATER, PLATE,
ARTISTIC INSPIRATION

Tip: You can expand your range of materials to include things like breadsticks, dips and cheese to give you more options.

Play pebble games

Yes – you read that right. All you need to play these games are pebbles. Who knew that small, round stones could be so exciting, eh?

Pebble race

This is a race where you have to make it as quickly as possible to the finish line while holding a pebble between your knees. If you drop it – you have to go back to the start.

Warning: it will make anyone who plays look like they are desperate for the loo!

YOU WILL NEED:
PEBBLES, 2 OR MORE PLAYERS

Pebble pétanque

Each player has two good-sized pebbles, but try to make sure they are different enough in colour or shape from your opponent's pebbles that you can tell them apart. Now take a smaller pebble (but large enough to be easily seen) which is called the "jack" and throw this some distance away.

You now take it in turns to stand in the same spot and try to get your stone as near as possible to the jack*. After you've thrown both your stones, run over and see who is the winner.

*If you can also knock your opponent's further away that is also useful – and gives you a good reason to gloat.

Fivestones

You're going to need… yes, that's right – five pebbles. How did you guess?

To begin, throw all five small pebbles into the air with one hand and then try to catch as many as possible on the back of the same hand (I know – tricky, right?) If you manage that, you then throw those you caught up again from the back of your hand and try to catch them in the palm of the same hand. If no pebbles are caught, your turn is over.

But if at least one pebble is caught you keep it in your hand and lay the other four on the ground. Now you need to toss this single pebble into the air, pick up one from the ground with the same hand before catching the stone you threw as well (and you thought it was tricky before!). If you manage it, put that stone aside, and try to do the

same, one at a time, with the other three stones on the ground.

And then, if you manage this, you can try picking up two at a time, then three, then four (now *there's* a challenge!).

Pebble football

This is a good way to make a walk more interesting. Everyone picks a pebble at the start and they must kick and dribble it all the way home without losing it along the way.

Hang ice mobiles

It's important to choose the right time of year to hang this mobile. In a cold winter you could be enjoying the sight of it for days, or even weeks, but in the summer you'll be lucky if it lasts until lunch.

First, lay out the cupcake moulds in a row in your plastic container and add some colourful berries or small evergreen leaves to each before sprinkling in some glitter.

Place a length of ribbon across all the moulds so it dangles into each and there is at least 30cm (12in) spare at one end. Now carefully pour water into each of the moulds until they are all full.

Ask a grown-up to put the container into the freezer overnight and then, when the water has frozen, press the ice shape out of each mould and admire its frozen beauty (but not while standing near a fire or radiator or that beauty won't last long).

Before it begins to melt, hang your ice mobile from an outdoor branch or hook. Try to find somewhere shady so it will last longer.

And if you haven't got any berries or leaves, why not add a drop or two of different food colouring to each mould so you have a line of colourful dangling jewels to hang?

YOU WILL NEED:
SILICONE CUPCAKE MOULDS, FLAT-BOTTOMED PLASTIC CONTAINER, SELECTION OF BERRIES OR LEAVES, SPARKLY GLITTER, RIBBON, WATER, SMALL JUG

Tip: Be aware that some berries can be harmful – NEVER put any in your mouth and always wash your hands after touching them.

Sow a grass head

You can of course make any character you wish for your grass head creation, although it is worth remembering this invaluable fashion advice: long green hair doesn't suit everyone.

If you choose to make an elf, first cut out a piece of green paper the same height as the toilet roll inner (you can use a ruler and pencil to check and mark this) and wide enough to wrap around the outside of the tube and then attach it using a glue stick.

Now use your ruler to measure another piece of paper, just as wide but half the height of the first. It could be dark green, red, brown, black or any colour really; elves are not very fussy about their trouser colour. After it's cut out, wrap it around the bottom half of the tube attaching it with a glue stick. When it's in place, draw a line down the lower half of the paper to make the two legs.

Next, cut out a long, slightly curved piece of paper or card with two mitten-shapes at both ends – this will form the arms). Attach it with some glue to the middle of your grass head's back, leaving the arms to move freely at the sides.

Cut out and decorate the face using pens, imagination and a little artistic flair before sticking it onto the tube.

Use some card to make the feet – these need an extra long section at the top which can be bent up and stuck to the inside of the tube with sticky tape.

Finish off with your own flourishes. You could use a long thin strip of paper to add a belt or how about using pom-poms for your elf's belt buckle?

Finally, take your empty yoghurt pot and fill it with cotton wool to just below the top. Soak this with water and then sprinkle on the grass seeds. If you slot this into the top of your decorated tube and place it on a sunny windowsill, you should see grass sprouting within a week.

YOU WILL NEED:
COLOURED PAPER OR THIN CARD, TOILET ROLL CARDBOARD TUBE INNER, RULER, PENCIL, SCISSORS, GLUE STICK, BLACK PEN, STICKY TAPE, DECORATIONS SUCH AS POM-POMS OR SEQUINS (OPTIONAL), SMALL ROUND YOGHURT POT (ABLE TO FIT INTO TOP OF TOILET ROLL INNER), COTTON WOOL, WATER, GRASS SEEDS

Tip: You can give your characters haircuts as the grass will happily regrow as long as it is kept watered.

Make savoury doughnuts

Repeat after me: not all doughnuts need to be sweet, not all doughnuts need to be sweet.

You don't look convinced.

Tell you what – why not just try it and see?

Start by making as large a circle as you can from your bread using the cookie cutter. If you don't have a cutter then you can put a mug on the bread and use a butter knife to cut away the bread around the edges instead.

Now use your finger to make a hole in the middle. You can pinch little bits of bread from around the inside edge until it has the correct doughnut shape.

For your coloured frosting, put a tablespoon of cream cheese into a bowl, add a few drops of food colouring and mix it together until you're happy with the shade. If you're making lots of doughnuts, add cream cheese to a separate bowl for each different colour and you'll have a selection to choose from.

And to make your sprinkles, use clean craft scissors to snip off bits from coloured pepper strips, sugar snap peas, salad onions or anything else you think will be a good topping.

Finally, you can construct your doughnuts by spreading your bread bases with the cream cheese frosting and then sprinkling on your savoury toppings.

Yum!

And do you know what would make the perfect pudding to follow?

A sweet doughnut!

YOU WILL NEED:
SLICED BREAD, ROUND COOKIE CUTTER OR MUG AND BUTTER KNIFE, CREAM CHEESE, SMALL BOWLS, FOOD COLOURING, CLEAN CRAFT SCISSORS, SELECTION OF VEGETABLES, PLATE

Tip: You can also use a halved bagel as the base for your doughnut or even a cored apple cut into slices.

Play paper plate ring toss

A quick reminder: when it comes to tossing plates as part of this game, it is very important that you only use *paper* versions. The alternative is very loud, very messy and will get you in so much trouble you may be grounded for a year.

Begin by making your targets. For each pole you will need a cardboard tube: the centre of kitchen rolls work well. Cut about 6–8 slits up from the base, each 2cm (¾in) long, bend these tabs outward and use sticky tape to attach them to the centre of a plate.

You can now use your paint and brushes to decorate the target. While the paint dries, you can make your hoops by bending a paper plate in half, snipping the middle to make a slit and then use this to start cutting out the centre of the circle. A single plate is quite light so you can use glue to join two hoops together to give them more weight before using the paint again to decorate.

When everything has dried you can set out your targets, perhaps writing on each one the points awarded for ringing it – with the targets further away netting you more than those closer. Now use something like a skipping rope or a scarf to make a line to stand behind. Every player has five rings to try and toss over the targets with the winner being the one who scores the most points.

YOU WILL NEED:
CARDBOARD TUBE, SCISSORS, STICKY TAPE, PAPER PLATES, PAINT AND PAINTBRUSHES, GLUE

Tip: If playing outside, you can use tall plastic bottles filled with water as targets and glue more paper plate hoops together to make them stronger and heavier.

Construct newspaper plant pots

YOU WILL NEED:
NEWSPAPER, SCISSORS, GLASS BOTTLE OR TALL JAR, DAMP CLOTH, COMPOST, SEEDS

Some plants, a bit like some people, don't really like the cold. That's why it helps to start growing them inside on a sunny windowsill until the garden warms up a little.

Of course, for this, you will need some pots, and if you fancy making a few of your own, all you need is an old newspaper.

Begin by opening out a large sheet and then fold down the top 12cm–15cm (5in–6in) – don't worry, you don't need to be too exact – and make a sharp crease. Open it up and cut along the line.

Now take your jar or bottle and place it on the newspaper ready to roll. Just make sure you leave enough newspaper free at the base so when you fold it, it goes just over halfway across the bottom of your jar or bottle.

Now roll the jar or bottle until the whole newspaper strip is tightly wrapped against it and then fold over the newspaper at the base so it is all neatly tucked under.

Tip: Use different sized bottles and jars to make smaller or larger pots.

Press the bottom of your jar or bottle against a hard surface to help make strong creases at the base and then place it on a damp cloth for about a minute (this will help the folded bottom to stay tucked under).

Now carefully slide out your jar or bottle, then bend over the top 2cm (¾in) inside the pot to help hold the edge.

Finally, fill your pot with some damp compost and sow your seeds in it. If you then place your pots on a tray of more damp compost, it will help the newspaper to stay moist and encourage the roots to eventually make their way through the sides.

Best of all, when the weather is warm enough to plant out your seedlings, you can simply place the whole pot in the ground as the newspaper will eventually just rot away.

Tip: You can also make a summery potpourri using dried flowers like rosebuds or petals, marigold flowers and lavender.

Concoct potpourri

If you've never heard of potpourri, it's something that makes your house smell delicious. So pretty much the opposite of children.

To make your own batch, you can begin by peeling an orange and then tearing the peel into pieces 2cm–3cm (¾in–1¼in) across. Lay these between sheets of kitchen roll and leave them to dry somewhere for 3–4 days. Or, you can just look under your bed and you'll probably find pieces that have been drying for far longer than this.

You can also find other interesting "treasures" to add to your potpourri when you're out and about – dried seed heads can look good or small pine cones. Just make sure you also let them dry for a day or so before you use them.

Now place all these dry ingredients in your bowl and begin adding your spices. Nutmeg is great, but to get a more intense smell it's best to break it up. Do this by placing it in a plastic bag, putting it on a chopping board, then hitting it with a rolling pin until it's in smaller pieces. Other good additions are cinnamon sticks snapped into sections, star anise, cloves and dry bay leaves.

When you're happy with the mix (and smell), put it in a glass jar. If you want to increase the scent you can also add some drops of an essential oil that complements your mix such as cinnamon. Now screw the lid on the jar, place it out of the sun and leave for a few days – giving it a shake every now and then to make sure all the items are soaking up the fragrance.

When you're ready to use the potpourri just pour it into a wooden or ceramic bowl and leave it somewhere it's needed as a "bad smell cover-upper" – like the loo.

You can also make it into a gift. Cut out one half of a plastic bag so you have a square, place your potpourri mix in the middle and then bring all the corners together to form a pouch. Use an elastic band to hold it together, tuck in a sprig of greenery, or maybe a cinnamon stick for decoration and then tie ribbon over the elastic band for a finishing touch.

Make peppermint creams

The good news is, if you don't like peppermint that's easily fixed: you can just change the flavouring you use. Unfortunately, "Make peppermint, orange, lemon or strawberry creams" was too long a title, so "Make peppermint creams" it is!

Start by sifting your icing sugar into a mixing bowl. Next you need to prepare your egg white. To separate it from the yolk you can carefully crack the egg into a bowl, then put in your (clean) hand to remove the yolk by lifting it up and letting the white drain through your fingers.

Now whisk your egg white until it is nice and frothy (but not stiff) and then add it to your icing sugar along with a teaspoon of peppermint essence and a few drops of food colouring. You need to mix it thoroughly until you are able to pull it together into a ball of fondant. If it's too dry, just add a teaspoon of water at a time until it is workable.

Tip your fondant onto a piece of baking paper sprinkled with icing sugar and knead it until it's nice and smooth. Next roll it out so it's about 1cm (½in) thick and then use small cookie cutters to make your sweet shapes. You can lay these on a fresh piece of greaseproof paper on a tray or plate.

Or if you haven't got a cutter, just roll pieces of the mixture into small balls that you can then flatten into discs. And if any of your shapes get a bit stuck, just use a flat butter knife to help move them off the paper.

While the creams are still soft, you can press in some edible decorations and then leave the sweets somewhere out of the way to dry for a couple of hours.

When they are dry, you could ask a grown-up to melt some chocolate that you can then dip half of your peppermint creams into for some delicious additional decoration.

YOU WILL NEED:
340G (12OZ) ICING SUGAR, 1 EGG WHITE, PEPPERMINT ESSENCE, FOOD COLOURING, WATER, EDIBLE DECORATIONS AND CHOCOLATE (OPTIONAL), SIEVE, MIXING BOWLS, WHISK, TEASPOON, BAKING PAPER, ROLLING PIN, SMALL COOKIE CUTTERS, GREASEPROOF PAPER, PLATE OR TRAY

Tip: You can split your
fondant mixture in
half before adding
your flavouring and
colouring to make two
different batches.

Play halt

This game needs to be played outside, otherwise things will get knocked over and grown-ups will be saying things far worse than "Halt!".

Everyone begins by standing around in a circle at the centre of which is a tea towel rolled up and tied together with string. The youngest player calls out a name at random and that person has to race to the centre and pick up the tea towel while everyone else scatters.

When the tea towel is in their hands they yell "Halt!" and everyone freezes. They now have three attempts to throw the tea towel and try to hit another player – if they're successful, that person is "it". But each time the tea towel falls to the floor other players are free to run again until the person who is "it" picks it up again.

174

If they fail to hit anyone after three goes, the player is out, but they do get to choose the next person to be "it". They also get to put their feet up and laugh every time someone gets hit with a rolled-up tea towel, so it's not all bad news.

Tip: You can also play this game with a soft ball.

Tip: For some double weather decorations, how about making a rainbow snowflake?

Thread snowflakes

Snowflakes are great, aren't they? Or at least they would be if they weren't so small and didn't disappear so fast. Still, you can sort that out with the help of a few beads and pipe cleaners.

Now although these are going to be bigger than normal snowflakes, we don't want to overdo it, so first you need to bend over each pipe cleaner and then cut it in half.

Take three of these halves to form your snowflake base. Twist the first two together by wrapping the first one around the middle of the second. Then do the same with the third pipe cleaner piece until you have formed a six-pointed star.

Now begin to thread the first of these points with beads. You could choose icy colours like blue and white, but as it's not actually in danger of melting there is nothing to stop you using hot and bright colours like red and orange instead. Whatever beads you choose, thread them on until you have filled up all but about the last 2cm (¾in) then bend this end over into a loop and push the end into the opening in the last bead. This will stop your beads falling off.

Thread beads on the other five points in the same way until the snowflake is completely decorated. If you want to display it in its non-melting, big-enough-to-see glory, then you can tie a piece of cotton to one of the points and stick the other to a window ledge or even a ceiling (with some grown-up help).

Play beach mini golf

This game of mini golf is going to take a *very* long time to play. Not because you are dreadful at golf (although, you may well be) but because before you even start you are going to need to build the course.

The good news is – building it is half the fun.

Begin by deciding where to place the course. You will need some damp sand as it holds its shape better and is easier for a ball to roll over. For that reason it's best to do this as the tide is going out: that way the sand is damp, but it will be a while before the tide turns and buries your brilliant course.

You can start with a relatively easy hole – that way players can get used to their clubs (or as we call them "spades") and golf balls (which look remarkably like tennis balls).

You can use a spade, a shell or even a finger to mark out the length of the hole – usually 2m–3m (2¼yds–3¼yds)) long works well with a larger "putting green" section at the end. To stop your ball rolling out of the course, make an edge of mounded sand and finally dig down to make your hole – the bigger the hole the easier it will be to put your ball in.

But this, of course, is only the start, you can make more and more elaborate holes. You could mound up sand and then dig a hole through with your hands to make a tunnel, create a mountain or volcano with steep sides and place the hole in the centre (now that is tricky). And, of course, you can create all sorts of obstacles in the way (sandcastles work well for this).

Tip: Keep testing out your holes by "putting" as you go to see how hard or easy they are in case you need to adjust them.

Make herbal bath bags

These make great gifts – especially for really smelly people (although it might be best not to mention this as you hand them your ever-so-thoughtful present).

Start by placing the large plate on your piece of muslin and draw around the edge with a pencil – or try a pen if this doesn't show up well enough. If you are using another sort of fabric, just test it

first to make sure water will pass through it

Now use the pinking shears to cut around the line. These sort of scissors make a pretty zigzag edge that helps to stop the fabric fraying.

When you have your circle, it's time to choose your herbs. You can use them fresh or dried and lavender, sage, rosemary, thyme, mint or bay

Tip: You can either float the bag in a bath or use the ribbon or band to tie your herb bag over the hot tap when it runs.

leaves all work well – just give them a sniff and decide which combination you like best.

When you have placed your selection in the middle, gather the edges of the fabric together and twist it around so the herbs are contained in the centre and then secure the fabric tightly with an elastic band.

For a finishing touch, tie a pretty ribbon over the elastic band to hide it and then, for an added flourish, you can slip a sprig or two of a herb under it for decoration.

YOU WILL NEED:
LARGE PLATE, PIECE OF MUSLIN OR SIMILAR FABRIC, PENCIL OR PEN, PINKING SHEARS, FRESH OR DRIED HERBS, ELASTIC BAND, RIBBON

Try water gun painting

If you read this and thought "Is that as much fun as it sounds?" then the answer is "Yes". And if your parents read this and think "Is that as messy as it sounds?" then the answer is also, very much "Yes!'"

You can get over this slight problem though by making sure you do this outside, in old clothes (or even swimsuits) and away from anything that could get stained (such as your parents).

The first job is to load your guns. Begin by making your paint. All you need to do is put equal amounts of paint and water into a jug and mix them thoroughly with a spoon. This is also best done outside if you can.

Now carefully pour the mixture into the water pistol chamber and put the stopper back in (if you have a really tiny opening then you can try adding this with a plastic syringe instead). Do this with a different colour for every water gun.

When your guns are ready, set up your paper. If you have an easel you can attach it to this with bulldog clips or to an old board leaning against a chair. You could even use drawing pins to attach it to a tree trunk.

And now it's time to get shooting. Sorry, I mean "begin your work of art". You can experiment by getting nearer or further away from the paper, trying shorter or longer shots and mixing up colours. Just remember, the paint is really supposed to end up on the paper… not on you.

Tip: If you don't have water guns you can use spray bottles.

YOU WILL NEED:
TEMPURA PAINT, WATER, OLD JUG AND SPOON, WATER GUNS, LARGE PIECE OF WHITE PAPER, EASEL AND BULLDOG CLIPS OR DRAWING PINS (OPTIONAL)

Create pebble pictures

There is nothing to stop you creating pebble pictures in your own back garden, but it's easiest to do this where you have lots of the art material to hand, so you know what that means?

No, not a pebble shop.

No, not a pebble supermarket either.

A beach, of course. The pebblier the better!

Sand is also good, or at least very fine stones, as this makes a great backdrop for your pebble picture.

And now all you need is some inspiration. If you want something simple to get you started, what about making some pebble footprints? These are easy to form with one large rounded stone for the sole and five smaller pebbles to make the toes.

If there are a few of you working on pictures, you could begin by searching out lots of different colours and sizes of pebbles that you can have close to hand to use for your artworks. You could even have your very own art gallery of different creations. Why not try forming some pebble creatures, or perhaps funny pebble faces, or what about a pebble house or even a pebble beach? Oh wait – that last one might be a bit too… pebbly. Tell you what, I'll leave the ideas up to you.

185

Make a nature tic-tac-toe

Stuck outside? Twiddling your thumbs? Think there's nothing to do? Well, you're wrong! I've got a perfect game for you to play. You just need to build it first.

Yes, tic-tac-toe or noughts and crosses is a simple game that is usually played with pencil and paper, but if you're outdoors and have nothing to write with, this is a useful alternative.

Begin by gathering sticks. You can either go for four long ones that you lay over each other to create the three-row, nine-box frame, or else just use 12 smaller twigs to create the same shape.

For your counters you'll need five for each player but they'll need to be very different from each other. You could use two very different types of leaves, or different coloured flowers or stones – or any combination of these.

And now you can play. It's very simple: players take it in turns to put one of their counters in one of the nine spaces. The first person to get three of their counters in a row, either horizontally, diagonally or vertically, wins the game.

If you're too well matched and keep tying, you can make things more interesting by setting up three tic-tac-toe sets you play at the same time. And if you call one the top level, one middle and one bottom, you can even play this as three-dimensional tic-tac-toe. Then again, if even the idea of this makes your brain ache, maybe you should stick with the original version.

Tip: If you make a larger stick frame, you can create a version where you aim to get four in a row instead.

Tip: Tie your frame together with twine if you want to use it again and again.

Play Billy goat splash

YOU WILL NEED:
STICKS OR STONES, TREASURE,
3 OR MORE PLAYERS

If you've not heard the story of the three Billy Goats Gruff, it is an endearing tale of smaller, weaker goats trying to save their own skin by encouraging a troll to eat their older brothers instead. Aahh. What a sweet story!

You can recreate something similar but with less threat to life, which is always good.

First, make your bridge by marking out a space with sticks or stones about 60cm (¾yd) wide and about 2m (2¼yds) long. At one end you need to leave a few pieces of treasure which can be anything you have to hand – pebbles, coins, toys. Now everyone else sits at the other end of the bridge as goats except for one player who is going to take the part of the troll. This person needs to sit with their back to the bridge and their eyes covered so they can't see the treasure or the other players either.

To play the game, goats have to take it in turn to cross over the bridge as quietly as possible and retrieve a piece of treasure each time. To disguise their "trip trapping" feet, the other goats make a lot of bleating noises, but if the troll thinks they can hear a crossing attempt they can shout "Splash!" and turn around. If any part of the goat is still on the bridge they are "captured" and have to sit with the troll (which is annoying, but not as bad as being eaten). But if there is no stray goat on his bridge the troll has to give up a piece of the treasure instead.

The game continues until the goats have taken all the treasure, or each of them has been captured by the troll. And the last surviving goat or the one who has retrieved the most treasure, gets to be the troll next time.

Tip: If you want to make it trickier, you can use "noisy" treasures!

Make a pomander

Pomanders may look very pretty but the very best thing about them is how they smell. Well, unless your top five lists of "stuff I really hate the smell of" includes both oranges and cloves, in which case this might not be for you.

If you're using a ribbon decoration then first stick on the double-sided sticky tape so it goes all the way around the orange from top to bottom (but keep the backing strip on). You can also add another two pieces of tape to intersect the first loop and divide the outside of your orange into quarters if you wish.

Now decide how you want to decorate your orange: you could follow the lines of the tape or how about adding a star, a face or even your own initial?

Mark out your pattern by puncturing holes in your orange every 0.5cm (¼in) using the nib of an old ballpoint pen, a wooden skewer or toothpick.

Push a clove into each hole – they should be next to each other but ideally not quite touching as they'll move nearer each other when the orange dries.

To finish, carefully remove the tape's backing strip and stick on your ribbon. If you are going for a "quartered" pattern, tie the ribbon together at the bottom and then loop back up to the top before tying another knot.

To help the oranges dry, you can pop them in an airing cupboard or somewhere else warm and dry for a few days, turning them occasionally. If they begin to look mouldy, throw them away, but if you have used plenty of cloves these act as a preservative and should keep that from happening. When they are dry, you can display them in a pretty bowl or even add a loop of ribbon so you can hang them up.

Tip: As the orange shrinks when it dries you may need to retighten the ribbon.

YOU WILL NEED:
MIXING BOWL, WOODEN SPOON, 2 PLATES, TABLESPOON, 75G (3OZ) OATS, 1 CARROT, FINELY GRATED (APPROX 50G/2OZ), 50G (2OZ) PEANUT BUTTER, 50G (2OZ) HONEY, 50G (2OZ) SULTANAS, GRATED ZEST OF HALF AN ORANGE, ¼ TEASPOON GROUND CINNAMON, 2 TABLESPOONS DESICCATED COCONUT

Mix carrot cake bites

These are a great snack, and as they have the word "carrot'" in the title you may even be able to fool grown-ups into thinking they are healthy. Then again, the word "cake" is a bit of a giveaway.

Simply put all the ingredients except the desiccated coconut in your mixing bowl and mix them together really well with a wooden spoon.

Next sprinkle the coconut onto one of the plates and put the other plate next to it.

Place a tablespoonful of the carroty mixture into your hand and shape it into a ball. Next, roll this around in the desiccated coconut until the outside is covered and put the finished "carrot cake bite" onto the clean plate.

Do this until all the mixture has been used (there should be enough for 8–10 carrot cake bites) and then put them in the fridge to chill and firm up for a good half an hour before tucking in.

Tip: If you find the mixture is a little too wet to shape into a ball then just add a few more oats, stir it together well and try again.

Tip: If you want to add a border to your card, cut about 1cm (½in) off the top and bottom of your piece of white card before you fold it in half and start cutting and decorating.

Make pop-up cards

It doesn't seem to matter what's being celebrated – a birthday, a wedding, exams being passed – we always seem to mark the occasion by… just sending a piece of folded card.

Well, you can improve that by about 100 per cent by sending a piece of folded card… that pops up. See! That's much more exciting.

There are lots of different versions you can create, but this design is good because it's super simple and you can adapt it in lots of ways.

Start by folding your plain white piece of card in half and then use pencil and ruler to measure and mark the lines (diagram 1). You can adapt these slightly in length but always make sure the longest line is less than half the total width or your pop-up will stick out beyond the edge of your folded card.

Now cut along these four lines and then fold back the three sections these form (diagram 2) to make creases. Carefully open the card and then "pop" out the three sections before folding the card shut again to put the creases in the right direction.

Now you have your three-tier base you can decorate it any way you choose – it's the perfect start for a cake, a pile of presents or even a fairytale castle. The key thing to remember is to make the pieces of paper you stick on slightly taller than sections of card you attach them to as this helps to hide the gaps between the tiers.

When you have all your decorations stuck on, fold your coloured piece of A5 card, glue the back of your white decorated card, line it up and stick it on. Then fold it shut and weight it down with books until the glue dries.

Now all you need to do is write your brilliant, inspired and creative message, such as "Happy Birthday".

Make a Pop Up Card

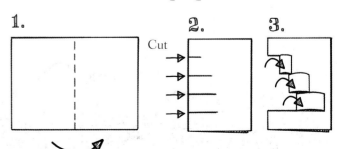

1.

2. Cut

3.

195

Play the table present game

You know those big family get togethers where grown-ups think it's a great idea for everyone to just sit around a table and talk? Well you're about to make them a *lot* more interesting.

First, you need everyone to bring a present. The rule is they should cost little or nothing (homemade and recycled gifts are always good) but they do need to be wrapped. Oh, and for smaller children it might be worth the adults providing their gift.

Now everyone places their presents in the centre of the table and two plastic cups are passed out, each with a dice inside.

On "go" the two people with cups use them to shake and roll their dice, before passing them onto the person on their left who goes next.

If anyone rolls a 6, they can choose a present from the centre of the table. And when all the presents have been taken, things really start to get interesting. Someone sets a timer for five minutes (or longer if you choose) and you begin again, only this time, if you roll a 6, you can "steal" a present from someone else. The only rule is you're not allowed to take a child's last present or they may cry. You can, however, steal an adult's last present – they may also cry, but hey, it's a tough world when you're a grown-up.

When the timer goes, the game ends and everyone can open any present they have managed to hold on to.

YOU WILL NEED:
PEOPLE AROUND A TABLE,
WRAPPED PRESENTS, 2 PLASTIC
CUPS, 2 DICE, TIMER

Tip: This is a great way to liven up the end of a Christmas dinner.

Create garden art

Now let's face it – nature is already pretty good at this whole artistic thing, but in most gardens it is a bit limited. Oh look, it's made a flower, and a tree, and there's a flower and what's that? Oh yes, I do believe it's another tree! But actually there are all sorts of potential artworks waiting to happen – nature just needs to borrow a bit of your creativity.

You can begin by looking carefully at what the garden – or park – or hedgerow – has to offer. Different leaves offer a huge variety of shapes – flowers can give you all sorts of colours, and then there are seedpods or berries, sticks or stones. When you start looking closely, you'll begin to see that nature is basically a very generous art store.

And when you've gathered your raw materials, you just need to decide what you will create – crazy aliens, giant dragons, amazing pets. Just try to avoid making trees. Nature's usually got that covered in the garden.

Tip: If you make a picture you want to keep, why not press the flowers and leaves? Do this by placing them for a couple of weeks between sheets of paper pressed down by heavy books and then stick them onto paper to recreate your picture.

Make a memo board

Memo boards are a great way to make sure you don't forget the important things in life: present ideas for your birthday, ice cream flavours you still need to try, all the ways you can wind up your brother.

To make one you first need an old picture frame. Ideally try to use one that has an acrylic rather than a glass front section as this is safer. But if you do use a glass frame, just make sure a grown-up is on hand to help.

Take the back off the picture frame and remove any picture that is in there. Now place the back of the frame on the wrapping paper and draw around it with a pencil. Try and choose a paper that isn't too dark as you need to be able to see your lists against this background.

Cut out the paper and then decide if you want to add a permanent heading to your list such as "Things to do" or "My birthday list" or even "Ways to annoy people" – it's up to you. If you use stencils for this you can make sure it's nice and neat, or just draw it on lightly with pencil until you are happy with the design and then go over it with a dark pen.

When the writing is dry, put the sheet of paper in the frame and replace the back. Finally, put a Velcro dot on the side of your frame and the other half on your dry erase marker so you can attach it to the memo board. That way, when you have a new genius idea for a way to annoy your brother, you won't waste time searching for a pen.

Tip: You can decorate your dry erase marker with washi tape.

TO DO...
clean fish
tidy bedroom

Plait wool dolls

Wool may make fine jumpers and scarves, but it's also ideal for legs, heads and arms – at least if you're making a doll.

To start your creation, first find a piece of card or a small notebook to wrap the wool around. And remember, whatever you choose will be the same height as your finished doll.

You will need to wrap your wool around it between 30 and 50 times. The taller the card or book, the more times you should wrap it.

When you're done, slide the wool off your card or book and then cut across all the fibres – so you're left with a bunch of wool all the same length.

Twist this bunch in the middle and bend it in half, then take a short length of wool and tie it tightly with a knot just below the twisted section before cutting off any long ends. This will form the head.

You can now leave most of the wool in the middle, but separate two equal sized bunches to form the arms. These need plaiting (see page 62 for instructions) and then tying with another piece of wool when you feel they are long enough. You can trim the ends to make "hands".

Now tie another length of wool around the large middle bunch to form a waist.

If you leave the doll like this, the wool will form a skirt. Or you can split it into two equal sized

YOU WILL NEED:
WOOL, PIECE OF STIFF CARD OR A SMALL NOTEBOOK, SCISSORS

bunches. If you plait these separately and finish them as you did for the arms, these will make legs and feet.

And, of course, you should feel free to personalize your dolls. You could pull some strands out from the head to make hair, or perhaps you could plait pieces of wool and then add them to make a crown, or a tie or a belt.

Tip: You can use different colours of wool to create contrasting features for your dolls.

Make drawer dividers

YOU WILL NEED:
OLD CEREAL AND FOOD BOXES,
PENCIL, RULER, SCISSORS,
WRAPPING PAPER, GLUE

This project will make your room tidier, but please don't let that put you off. Instead, let's focus on the fact that you're going to have to get through loads of cereal before you can begin. Feel better? Good.

Take the drawer you want to organize and place your empty boxes in it until it's nice and full. Of course, the boxes will all be too tall so the first job is to cut them down to size. Place each one up against the side of the drawer and use a pencil to mark all the way around where it is in line with the top edge. Take out each box and go over these lines neatly with a ruler and pencil before using your scissors to cut where you have marked before putting them back in the drawer to check it will still close easily.

To decorate each compartment, first draw around the bottom of the box on the back of your pretty wrapping paper. Now use your ruler to make this shape longer – long enough to go along the bottom twice and up and down the sides too (see diagram 2) and then cut it out.

Glue the paper in the middle and place it inside the box, using your fingers or the bottom of a pencil to press it down and into the bottom edges. Use more glue to stick it down on the outside too (see diagram 3).

Now lay the box down and drawn around the largest side on more wrapping paper. Again, use your ruler to enlarge the shape so it will be long enough to cover the last bare sections of the box. Cut it out and then glue it down as you did before.

When you have done this for all your boxes, you can place them inside the drawer ready to tidy and organize all your things.

Sorry about that.

Lining your boxes

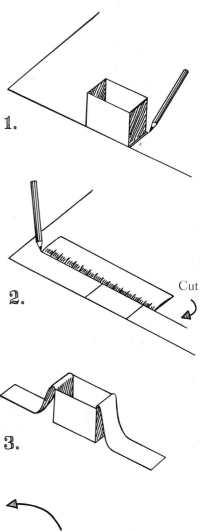

1.

2. Cut

3.

Tip: You can add cut-down toilet roll inners to fit inside larger boxes to add more compartments.

Make junk models

This activity should prompt a round of applause from your parents – after all, you are being creative *and* you're recycling! However, you might want to explain all this to them first otherwise they will simply think you have emptied the bin onto the kitchen table.

You see, that's the thing with junk modelling – you're going to be using an awful lot of rubbish. In fact, it's worth collecting together plenty of things before they are thrown out, such as old cereal packets, egg boxes, plastic bottles, cardboard tubes and loo rolls, shoeboxes, lids, corks – and anything else that catches your eye.

If you have a plan for what to make, then you could look out for specific things to build it with, but it can be just as much fun to make something up on the spot.

Masking tape is incredibly useful as it will hold things together and can also be painted over if you want to decorate your finished creation. Glue and staples are good for attaching paper and card. Oh, and a winning smile is great for keeping parents on board.

Tip: You can supplement your junk modelling supplies with other useful crafting items such as tinfoil, cocktail sticks, kebab skewers, pipe cleaners, tissue paper, beads and pom-poms.

Fold a money shirt

YOU WILL NEED:
PAPER MONEY

So… okay… you don't have to use paper money for this – you could just fold a piece of paper. But shhh, don't tell the grown-ups or they'll stop passing over large amounts of cash.

First, fold up the bottom third of the note (diagram 1). Now turn it over (diagram 2) and fold this rectangle in half, unfold (diagram 3) and then fold in both sides so they meet at the middle line (diagrams 4–5).

Take the section that has the extra flaps, lift them up from the centre and fold each one out at an angle (diagrams 6–7) so part of the triangle sticks out over the sides (these will be the shirt sleeves).

Turn it over and check you are happy with the shirt sleeves and then take the very top edge of the note and fold it down about 0.5cm (¼in) (diagram 8).

Turn your note over again and now fold in the two top corners at an angle so the points meet on the middle line to make a collar (diagrams 9–10).

Now bend the note upwards so you tuck the top of the shirt underneath the collar and then press it flat (diagrams 11–12).

Finally, smile adorably in the hope that the owner of the bank note will be so impressed they gift it to you.

Or cry.

Whatever works best.

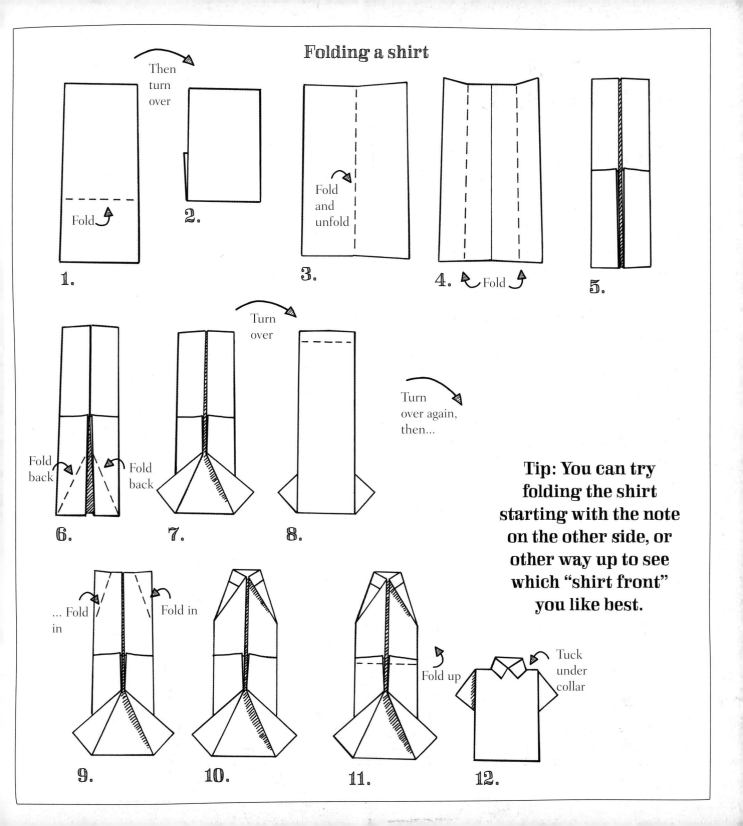

Hold a night-time treasure hunt

YOU WILL NEED:
1 OR MORE HUNTERS/SEARCHERS, TREASURE, TINFOIL, TORCHES

Tip: Grown-ups might want to make a note of where they have hidden the treasure just in case you can't find it. After all, we wouldn't want the chocolate getting lost, would we?

You can use any treasure you like for this hunt, but I would seriously recommend chocolate. Then again, I always seriously recommend chocolate, so that's no surprise.

When you have chosen your treasure (it's chocolate, right?), wrap it in tinfoil and then, just before it gets dark, ask a grown-up to go and place it in the garden. Just make sure it isn't hidden behind or underneath anything or it's going to be almost impossible to find.

When it's dark, wrap up warm, grab a torch each and head outside to start searching the garden for your treasure. You'll need to keep sweeping your torch side to side, and up and down, and keep a close eye out. Because the foil is reflective it should look very shiny when the torchlight hits it, allowing you to spot (and then eat) the treasure.

And, of course, it's even more fun to have lots of different treasure (or chocolate) hidden around the garden so the hunt can go on for a while.

Resources

UK

Argos
Online or high street shops good for items such as balls, paddling pools, torches, hula hoops and play sand.
argos.co.uk | 0845 6403030

Baker Ross
Huge range of craft accessories including paper, card, paints and brushes, sticky tapes, scissors, glue, beads, buttons, lollipop sticks, chalks, glitter, string, googly eyes, ribbon, pipe cleaners, velcro dots and marker pens.
bakerross.co.uk | 0844 576 8922

B&Q
Wide selection of supplies including compost, garden hoses, plant pots, seeds, strings, PVC pipes, bricks, paint rollers, spades and forks. Also good for paint, duct tape, masking tape and washers.
diy.com | 0845 609 6688

Dunelm Mill
Useful for fabric, oilcloths, thread and wool, as well as household items like funnels, measuring jugs, battery tealights and cupcake moulds.
dunelm-mill.com | 0845 1656565

Garden centres
Good all year round sources of gardening supplies, seeds and plants. You can find local centres by searching The Garden Centre Association
gca.org.uk | 0118 930 8918

Lakeland
Useful for household supplies such as kebab skewers, food colouring and flavouring, straws, graters, wooden spoons and muffin tins.
lakeland.co.uk | 01539 488100

Pharmacies
Often good places to find essential oils, cotton wool, face and body lotion and petroleum jelly. Find your local one at: pharmacyregulation.org/registers/pharmacy | 0203 713 8000

Ryman
Good for stationery items including tracing paper, card, glue etc as well as playing cards.
ryman.co.uk | 0800 801901

Wilko
Good value household items such as jugs, bowls, wooden spoons, cupcake moulds and timers. Also good for craft and garden supplies in season.
wilko.com | 08456 080807

AUSTRALIA

Big W
Craft and game supplies.
bigw.com.au | 1300 244 999

Bunnings Warehouse
Garden supplies and household items from bamboo canes to tea lights.
bunnings.com.au | (03) 8831 9777

Kmart
Home, game and garden supplies.
kmart.com.au | 1800 124 125

USA

Target
Accessible household supplies, from essential craft kits to stationery and games.
target.com | 1-800-591-3869

Michaels kids
Creative screen-free supplies for crafty afternoons.
michaelskids.com | 1-800-642-4235

Blitsy
Wide range of craft supplies from painting tools, markers, accessories and more.
blitsy.com | (855) 813-3429

Categories

Projects done in minutes

Projects in an hour or less

Longer projects

Good for spring

Good for summer

Good for autumn

Good for winter

Good for parties or bigger groups

Good for younger children (4–7 years)

Good for older children (8–11 years)

Craft projects

No mess activities

Best for Cooks

Best for tricksters

Best for artists

Perfect for presents

Great games

Paper folding projects

Outdoor games

Outdoor activities

Index

Acknowledgements

It is misleading to have simply one name on the cover because this book owes its existence to many more people and here I get a chance to thank them all.

Firstly to Tara O'Sullivan, my wonderful editor over the last three '101s', who is so scarily organized that she makes the complex task of getting a book published look like a walk in the park.

I'm indebted to Louise Leffler who has, yet again, created a beautiful looking book and Sarah Leuzzi, whose illustrations make me smile every time.

And it has been a pleasure to work alongside Kate Whitaker once more – our wonderful photographer who manages to capture the fun in each project she shoots. To help in this task, Kate was gifted with some brilliant models: Aiden, Albert, Archie, Azalea and Merryn, Eddie and Ellen, Esme and Finan, Florence, Isaac and Jake, Fox and Tallulah, Jessica and Joseph, Johnny, Katie and Josh, Lauren, Isobel and Hugh, Lottie and Maddie, Naomi and Lucas, Mason, Mawgan and Amelie, Miles and Blake, Oliver, Oscar and Rosalind, Oscar and Iris and Willow. A huge thank you to all of you for bringing the book to life.

Finally, I must thank my family who once more have supported me brilliantly. To "Granny" and "Grandma" for stepping in whenever they were needed, to Ava, Oscar and Archie for being my "screen-free testers" and the inspiration behind the books, and Reuben – the best decision I ever made. I love you all.

(Not sure? Go to page 66 to work it out.)